A Practical Guide to
NEEDLE LACE

We will never achieve the impossible, let it be our lantern.

RENÉ CHAR (1907–1988)

Cover design by Brenda McCallum
Type set in Sabon LT Std/FairplexNarrowBook

ISBN: 978-0-7643-5869-2
Printed in China
5 4 3 2

FSC
www.fsc.org
MIX
Paper from
responsible sources
FSC® C167893

Published by Schiffer Publishing, Ltd.
4880 Lower Valley Road
Atglen, PA 19310
Phone: (610) 593-1777; Fax: (610) 593-2002
E-mail: Info@schifferbooks.com
Web: www.schifferbooks.com

For our complete selection of fine books on this and related subjects, please visit our website at www.schifferbooks.com. You may also write for a free catalog.

Schiffer Publishing's titles are available at special discounts for bulk purchases for sales promotions or premiums. Special editions, including personalized covers, corporate imprints, and excerpts, can be created in large quantities for special needs. For more information, contact the publisher.

We are always looking for people to write books on new and related subjects. If you have an idea for a book, please contact us at proposals@schifferbooks.com.

A Practical Guide to
NEEDLE LACE

JACQUELINE PETER

SCHIFFER
PUBLISHING

4880 Lower Valley Road • Atglen, PA 19310

Contents

Preface

I would first like to pay tribute to my late husband, Michel Jourde, designer and creator of bobbin lace cards and Un des Meilleurs Ouvriers de France,* and lacemaker at the Atelier Conservatoire national de la dentelle since its creation because it would have given him great pleasure to write this preface for Jacqueline's book.

Michel, a talented artist, helped make lacework more modern without forgetting the quality of the work and the fundamental principles of this ancient technique.

He was Jacqueline's teacher—she was a remarkably talented student and won first prize in the Victoires de la dentelle at Puy-en-Velay in 1995, for her reproduction in lace of a black-and-white cinema poster.

She continues her legacy, notably through her magnificent sketches for both bobbin and needle lacework.

Since receiving her teaching qualification in Bruges in 2006, with her thesis "Creators of Lace in the Haute-Loire from the 17th to the 21st Centuries," Jacqueline teaches both lacework techniques. Needle lace is an area that doesn't have many books written about it. The book you are holding is a rich introduction to this technique and makes up for this lack of information and imparts the knowledge of a true needle lace lover.

Jacqueline's goal is for you to understand the technique as a whole and to show you the almost infinite range of possibilities. You will find this clear and precise book a valuable learning tool.

Hélène Jourde

*Un des Meilleurs Ouvriers de France is a prestigious craftsman competition held every four years in France.

Foreword

A designer by trade, I first discovered bobbin lace several years ago. Later, having been taught how to design lacework on card by Michel Jourde, a lacework designer and Un des Meilleurs Ouvriers de France, I did a course to become a lacework teacher; the course included a needle lace apprenticeship at the Kantcentrum in Bruges with Geneviève Leplat and Hilda Vrijsen as teachers. It was a wonderful experience!

I think that every lacemaker should have some knowledge of needle lace. It's part of our training in the domain of different stitches.

This book is for anyone just beginning or for those who want to improve their technique, thanks to numerous sketches and photos. Apart from a few variants, the lacework stitches I use in this book are similar to those used in Alençon lace, even if the term "Point d'Alençon" is reserved for locally made items using very fine thread.

Although this book does not include all stitches, it does include the main ones. I learned them during my training; I discovered others in books and later tried them out. They constitute the basis of everything that characterizes needle lace. At the end of the book you will find various models of increasing difficulty. They have step-by-step explanations that will be a useful guide as you progress.

I hope this book will help all lacemakers express themselves through their personal work.

Introduction

There are only two ways of making lace, with bobbins or with a needle. The first lacework, according to if it was bobbin-made or done with a needle, was called "lace" or "braid." It was mainly used as borders, with a preference for the outer edges cut and called "lace edging."

Whether you use a needle or bobbins, they aren't two different objects but two aspects of the same product. However, we have fallen into the habit of calling certain bobbin-made stitches "points": point de Paris, point de Lille, etc. Lacework made with these stitches therefore takes on the same name (e.g., Paris lace, Lille lace). It is impossible to try to change established customs. Thus, to avoid any confusion, we use the terms "bobbin lace" and "needle lace."

Bobbin lace is created by weaving, often braiding numerous threads. The threads are fixed to the frame by pins on one side and bobbins on the other. The bobbin is moved, passing over or under its neighbors, thus intertwining the threads.

Needle lace is carried out on a piece of parchment or paper that has the pattern drawn on it. The "frame," also called a cordonnet, which serves as the support for the loops, is couched round the outline of the pattern. In this way, the pattern is reproduced in thread, fixed to the paper.

Row by row, the loops are fixed to the cordonnet to create needle lace.

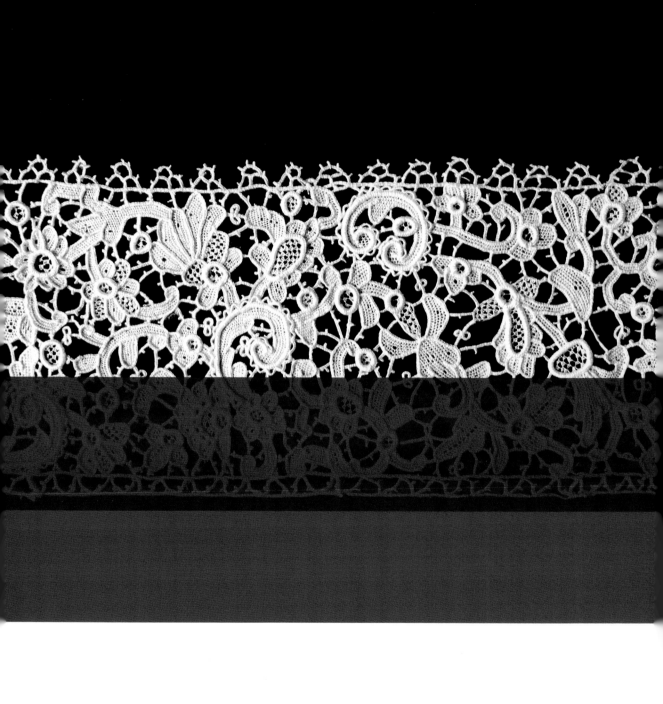

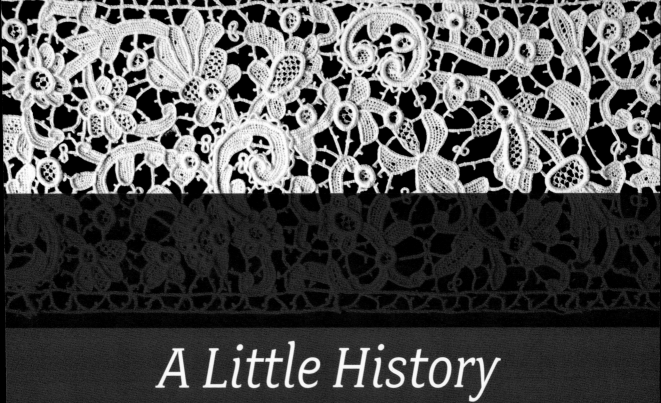

A Little History

From Embroidery to Lacework

Nets, which have been used since antiquity for hunting and fishing, can be embroidered, even decorated with pearls and used as clothing. Nets embroidered using linen stitch and filled using darning stitch, attributed to France, was the first step toward lacework. It is made up of square meshes knotted at the corners.

Filet lace using a meshing needle (or shuttle)

Filet lace

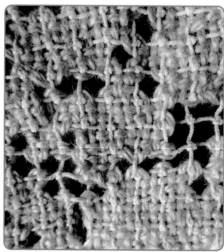

Details of filet lace

In Europe at the end of the fifteenth century emerged elaborate whitework embroidery intended mainly for house linen. During the second half of the 16th century, this style of embroidery began to be used in clothing and soon became widespread.

The beginnings of the invention of needle lace can without doubt be attributed to a seamstress who, wanting to highlight the aspect of whitework embroidery, had the idea of clearing the linen here and there by creating small gaps.

DRAWN-THREAD EMBROIDERY

From this discovery came drawn-thread embroidery (now called "withdrawn ground" or "jours"), which consists of removing the threads from the linen in both directions, to leave gaps and then recovering the remaining threads by relief embroidery. Constantinople is often cited as being the origin of drawn-thread work.

PULLED-THREAD EMBROIDERY

To accentuate the transparent effect, the threads are not removed from the linen but are pulled aside, tightened by a knot and kept in place by silk thread to separate them from the others. In this way we create a sort of canvas. The reserved linen is embroidered and forms the décor.

CUTWORK EMBROIDERY

To increase the importance of the spaces, pieces of the linen are cut out with scissors. The remaining threads are then stitched back into the embroidery by using darning, overcast, or buttonhole stitch. This is cutwork embroidery. In the second half of the sixteenth century, geometrical shapes began to replace the usual flowers, leaves, foliage, animals . . .

Cutwork embroidery

RETICELLA

Another technique was created at the same time, reticella. Taken from drawn-thread and cutwork embroidery, it consists of removing almost all the threads from the linen, in both directions. The remaining threads are twisted around the needle, forming the limits of the decorative area. Within these squares you will see crossed and diagonal threads, allowing the creation of roses and diverse other patterns.

Reticella   *Reticella (sixteenth-century sample book)*

PUNTO IN ARIA (STITCH IN THE AIR)

This very elaborate form of cutwork embroidery, with its geometric designs, precedes needle lace. This stitch came from the desire to create a border similar to the lacy edges obtained with bobbin lace. To create them, seamstresses worked without the linen. The seamstress made only the border on a piece of parchment festooned to the frame, and then decorated with different stitches: this is *punto in aria* (stitch in the air).

The fundamental difference between this and the cutwork technique is that the latter is dependent on the linen, while stitch-in-the-air work is carried out on a frame, separate from its support and therefore independent of the linen. The result is pure lace. This border is then sewn onto the reticella.

Mixed Technique

Each technique creates a unique result. Bobbin lace generally results in a flatter effect, while needle lace clearly highlights the outlines of the patterns.

These two techniques can coexist in the same work. For example we find needle lace patterns appliquéd to a backdrop created by bobbin lace, called "drochel" (a Flemish term that designates a background created by bobbin lace). This ground, reserved for application, was made up of bands of 3 or 4 centimeters joined by an invisible seam. These patterns were mounted by a specialized worker called a "striqueuse" in Belgium (the worker who performs the main process in the creation of lace). This enabled the creation of large pieces, such as veils for brides.

Example of mixed lace (private collection). On the right of the dress's border, the needle lace flower has already been integrated, while to the left, it is still waiting to be placed.

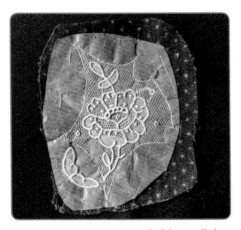

Detail of the needle lace

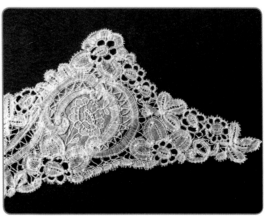

Detail of the two laceworks (needle lace and bobbin lace) assembled

Needle Lace through the Ages

Although Italy seems to have been number one in the lacework industry, the invention of lace has been attributed to other countries as well.

In France, it was only in the fifteenth century that lace began to appear on clothes in various portraits. During the Renaissance, lacework became an important and productive industry, mainly in Italy, France, and Belgium, which count among the biggest manufacturers of needle lace.

France imported large quantities of Flemish and Italian lace. As a result, several sumptuary laws were attached to lace, which had become a luxury as expensive as the cloth and trimmings made of gold, silver, or silk thread. The first ruling dated back to 1629, and up to thirty-two others followed soon after. One dated 1660, which forbade wearing any imported laces, caused a lot of flutter: a satire in verse called "La révolte des passements" was written by a group of fashionable ladies who frequently met at the Hotel de Rambouillet.

BIRTH OF THE ALENCON STITCH

Finally, in 1665, to put a stop to the colossal fortunes spent on these "frivolities" that poured coin into foreign coffers, Colbert, who was the minister of finance under Louis XVI and superintendent of buildings and manufactories, created the manufacture of French lace, with a nine-year monopoly.

With the frontiers now closed, foreign lace makers were invited to pass on their knowledge. Flemish and Venetian laces were the most popular and the most expensive, and they were by far the favorites in all the European royal courts. French lace therefore had to overcome its rivals and replace them.

Around twenty towns within the French realm were chosen for their solid lace-making traditions in both needle lace and bobbin lace. Twenty Venetian lacemakers were hired to come and teach their technique.

In Alençon, Jacques Prévost and Marie Ruel, in charge of setting up this first factory, had the responsibility of putting together the principal agreements.

Lace makers should work exclusively for the factory, no matter the technique, and follow designs and patterns made exclusively in France. This provoked anger, fraud, and resistance, which in turn were followed by raids and fines.

From the moment when the factory in Alençon first held the monopoly, the name "point de France" (chosen by Madame de la Perrière) applied only to the needle lace technique.

At the end of the nine-year monopoly, Alençon lace stood out so well that no other measure was necessary to ensure its supremacy. In fact, it called for extremely precise knowledge, comprising at least ten steps of creation that needed the same number of workers.

Later, the point de France was renamed "point d'Alençon."

DURING THE REVOLUTION

In 1685, the revocation of the Edit de Nantes by Louis XIV caused Huguenot lace makers to flee the country. However, most of the people who lived and worked in Alençon were Catholics, and so their knowledge remained in the town.

In 1757, most of the point d'Alençon factories were still owned by the descendants of those who had opened them in the time of Madame de la Perrière.

Before the Revolution, between 6,000 and 7,000 women worked in the factories for eighty merchants and manufacturers. After the Revolution, in 1880, there were only twenty-seven manufacturers left, and the number of workers continually decreased.

One after the other, the factories closed down. Only five manufacturers struggled through the crisis. The Napoleonic Wars had ruined Germany, Russia, and all of northern Europe, where the point d'Alençon had most of its outlets.

In France, the point was worn only in winter. But the absence of the emperor and his court during several winters reduced the sales to nothing.

Tracing and its matching lace, point d'Alençon Lefébure flounce. Founded in 1829 in Bayeux, the Lefébure House mostly produced bobbin lacework until 1855, when it turned to needle lace.

At the same time, tulles and blondes (bobbin lace made with natural-colored silk or gold or silver thread) began to replace the point and had several advantages: they were good imitations, they were less expensive because they were machine made, and they made the middle-income people who wore them look rich. It was therefore decreed that such imitations were forbidden in the court to help preserve the point and its sales.

Finally, to promote this French luxury, international expositions were held where lace work had a prominent place.

In 1875, the manufacturer Jules Huignard set up a lacework school within his factory. This meant that he could take advantage of the best workers, guaranteeing the quality of the point.

The most important item to be made in his factory was a dress ordered by Empress Eugénie, copied from the pattern of a dress worn by Madame de Pompadour.

Vellum from Empress Eugénie's wardrobe, nineteenth century (J. Huignard's flourish and initials are visible on the vellum; Alençon Museum)

Flounce representing the cornucopia, nineteenth century (from J. Huignard's workshop; Alençon Museum)

TWENTIETH CENTURY

The rich backers had disappeared, and needle lace was hardly in fashion since its cost couldn't compete with that of bobbin lace and even less with mechanically made lace.

In 1938, the chamber of commerce reorganized the lacework school, which was called the Soeurs de la Providence.

In 1965, the Association La dentelle au Point d'Alençon was created, which ran the school and its museum. But sales no longer covered salaries, and the school closed in 1974.

On November 16, 2010, point d'Alençon lace was added to UNESCO's Intangible Cultural Heritage. From 2012 until today, a dozen or so lacemakers continue the tradition and maintain the technique.

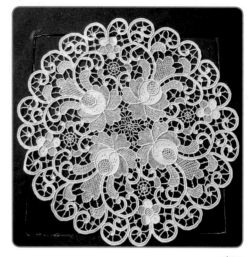

Burano lace

Bridesmaid's veil created by lacemaker Corine Santon (Alençon Museum, lent by the Mobilier National)

Principal Needle Lace Work

ITALY

Venetian point plat: Its elements are spread out without any logical order. Around 1640, the point plat used the same ornamental forms as the Gros Point de Venise. Their difference lies in the absence of embroidery.

It is reasonably inexpensive and can be gathered. The patterns are joined by brides that were replaced in the eighteenth century by hexagonal meshes.

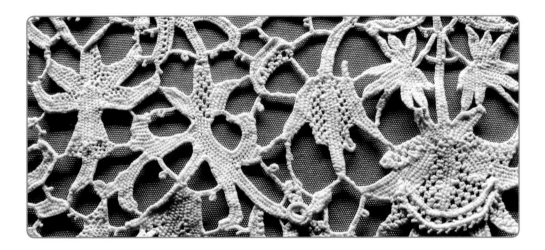

Point de Burano: Its ground is formed by thick squares perpendicular to the edge. The brides with picots are elaborate and the filling regular, with numerous modes

and a large number of fancy points. The Point de Burano is used in clothes and accessories, as well as in fans, parasols, table linen, etc.

Gros Point de Venise: The motifs are placed side by side and joined by bands or brides with picots. The embroidery consists of around fifty threads, which gives it a sculptural character. Its beauty lies in its large variety of fillings. Worn flat, it is seen on collars or lapels on both religious and secular clothing.

Point de Venise à la Rose: A more refined and feminine lace, its motifs and foliage became smaller by the end of the seventeenth century. The reliefs look like snowflakes, which is why in France it is called "point de neige."

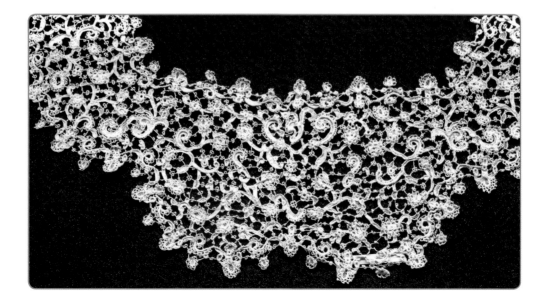

FRANCE AND BELGIUM

Point d'Alençon: It is the only lace that carries the name "point de France." All the patterns are realistic representations of ferns and peonies. Different fillings and modes are used.

Point de Argentan: This point progressively succeeded the point de France. Its brides were replaced by a ground of hexagonal meshes.

Point de Sedan: This lace uses symmetric motifs; its decors are on a background of hexagonal brides.

Brussels Point (also called "Point de Gaze"): Its needlepoint motifs are appliquéd to a "drochel" background (see page 17).

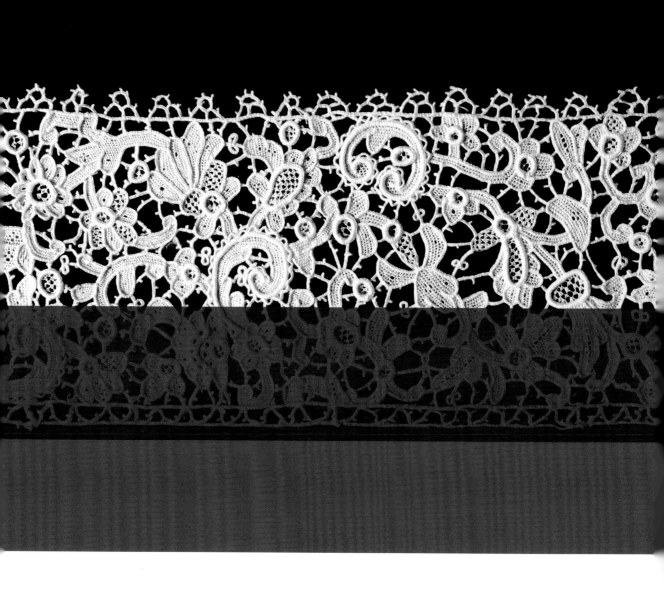

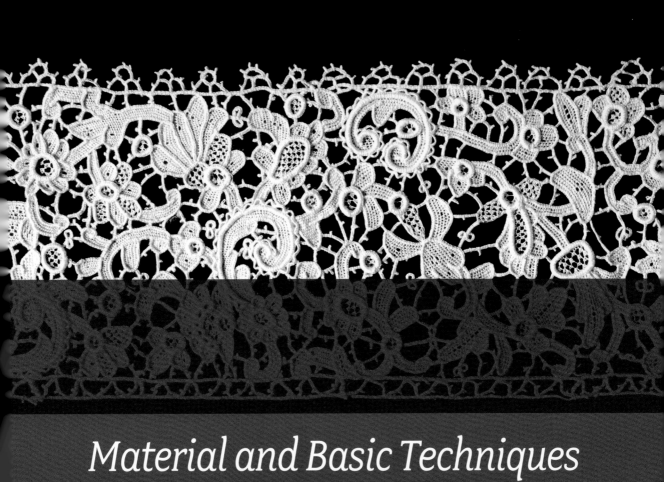

Material and Basic Techniques

Material

Before starting to do lacework, you will need some materials. Most of the items in the following list can be found in craft stores.

Keep close by:

- A full-size copy of the pattern you want to make

- Two pieces of cloth (or one folded in two), not too thick and preferably cotton. They will be used as a support for the lace and should be larger than the pattern by a few centimeters on each side

- Adhesive plastic (mat) which will protect the lace from pattern's ink

- Sewing needles no. 8 and no. 10, according to the fineness of the work

- Tacking thread for the frame: usually we use tacking thread no.100 or 120 *Brok*

- Working thread (the thread that will make up the lace): Brok 36/3 cotton thread is ideal to begin with, but other threads can be used (see the box below). It's best not to use synthetic thread.

- Horsehair to thicken the top stitches. Mane hair is best. Used bowstrings from a lutemaker will also work. But first wash them carefully with soapy water. Horsehair can be replaced by metallic thread (you'll find an example on page 100)

- A tracing wheel to determine the location of the needle points on the pattern (it's mainly used at the beginning)

- A pricking needle and a pricking board (optional) to create the impact of the basting stitch in advance

Other Threads

Other than the Brok 36/3 cotton thread, you can create your lacework with the following:

- DMC 6-strand thread
- Silk thread
- Ariane 50 Egyptian cotton thread
- Kantklos Garen 60 Egyptian cotton thread
- DMC no. 80 special thread
- Cartier-Bresson no.100 Irish dimity thread

- A piece of plastic to avoid getting the work dirty

- A pair of embroidery scissors

- A lobster claw to smooth the finished work (instead of an iron). You can find a claw in any store that sells seafood.

- A thin crochet hook (no. 60), useful for holding on to the frame

- A razor blade to cut the lace from its support

- Tweezers for clearing away the last threads

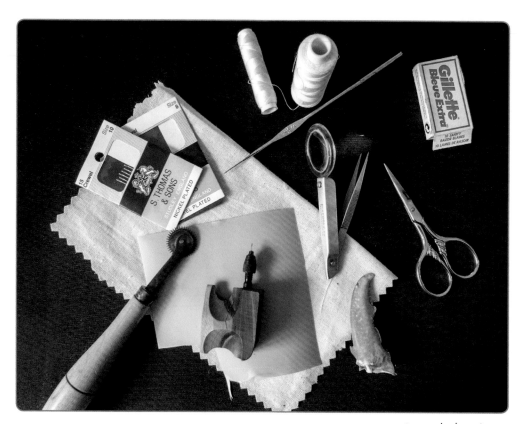

Lacemaker's equipment

Needle Lace Steps

The creation of needle lace is carried out according to a succession of precise steps. It is worked on the right side, contrary to bobbin lace, which is worked on the reverse side. These steps will be detailed in the following pages.

The choice of the design (pattern): This is reproduced in full-size onto a piece of paper, on which the lace will be directly worked.

The support: The design is then placed on two pieces of cloth (or one folded in two) covered by adhesive plastic. It is all tacked together.

Pricking: The model is then pricked all along the outline of the pattern. This step is for beginners; those who are used to lace work don't need to follow this step (it was indispensible when working on parchment, which is thicker and harder to pierce than paper).

The cordonnet: The cordonnet or "trace" is the pattern's outline reproduced in thread: it is the frame of the lace. Long ago, the seamstress who did the cordonnet was called the "traceuse."

The ground: This is the lace's background between the motifs (ground progressively replaced the brides in France).

The fillings: Used to fill the motifs, these stitches create shadowy effects.

The modes: This refers to fancy motifs that are ornamental in character, as opposed to fillings.

The brides: These join the motifs together.

Top stitching: This step is done once the ground, fillings, and modes are finished. Top stitching, using thicker thread, gives relief to contours and consolidates the lace.

Separating: The lace is detached from its support, using a razor blade.

Trimming: Removing all the stray bits of thread from the lace, using tweezers.

Smoothing: This last step consists of going over the fillings with a lobster claw (this replaced the wolf's tooth that apparently was once used!)

Carrying out these different steps (ground, fillings, modes, and top stitching, etc.) is what lacework is all about. All these steps will be detailed in the next chapter.

PHOTOS OF EACH STEP

1. The pattern

2. Pricking

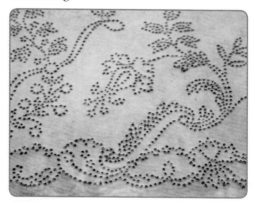

3. Cordonnet or "trace"

4. Ground

5. Fillings

6. Modes

CREATING THE PATTERN

A traditional needle lace pattern is drawn in ink on a simple sheet of paper. In the past, in addition to following current fashion, the artist had to respect the future use of his work.

The pattern was reproduced three times in a workshop:

- A copy of the original pattern (called the artistic design) was stored in the pattern file.

- A second copy of the same pattern was given to the lacemaker so that she could easily follow the pattern's curves, since these weren't always visible on the pricked parchment that was used as a support for the lace. The names of the points to be used were denoted by a single letter on this copy to make them easier to locate.

- A third copy was the technical design: the lines and contours of the artistic design were reproduced onto this copy to guide the creation of the cordonnet.

Nowadays, lace is no longer bound to the requirements of past centuries, and the choice of patterns is limitless. If you don't draw very well, you can choose a design that pleases you, as long as it isn't too difficult. In the last chapter of this book you will find several models that you can recopy to your heart's content.

To begin with, you will need only a sheet of paper on which you will reproduce the pattern of the lace you wish to create. A photocopy of the design is perfectly acceptable.

Simplify your pattern by avoiding superfluous details or overly pointed angles, which will automatically become rounded.

The lines should be even and not too thick because the cordonnet should be able to follow them easily.

Ancient pattern on tracing paper ready to be transferred onto paper. This needle lace model appears to have been drawn with the idea of eventually integrating it into a piece of bobbin lace.

Make three copies of your pattern: one you will directly work your lace on; on the second you will draw in arrows to mark the direction of the cordonnet and also add your choice of points.

Make a precise note of the cordonnet's direction. It's an operation that takes research and patience, but it will make your work easier later on since the top stitches will follow the same direction.

Dessin sur calque et sa réalisation en dentelle.

PREPARING THE SUPPORT

Lace is made on a support. Historically, this was done on parchment, which could be used several times, but it became too expensive and was replaced at the beginning of the twentieth century by fine mesh, whose suppleness made it easy to handle.

Therefore, your support will consist of the paper bearing your pattern (a simple rectangle here that you could use as your first sample) and two pieces of cloth placed under it (fig. 1). The sheet of paper is then covered by clear adhesive plastic, fixed directly to the pattern and overflowing onto the cloth. The whole thing is then tacked together using large stitches (fig. 2).

Fig. 1

Fig. 2

PRICKING

Long ago, lacemakers pricked their pattern beforehand, using a pricking needle and a pricking board, to prepare the impact of the tacking stitches.

This step is no longer completely necessary because the needle goes through cloth more easily than through parchment, which was once used as the support. However, pricking helps beginners determine where their tacking stitches will be, which should be 2 mm apart.

To help you get the right distance between stitches, you can use a tracing wheel as long as its teeth are no more than 2 mm apart. Run the wheel along the outlines of the pattern: the marks left by the wheel will help you keep your stitches even.

CORDONNET

The cordonnet or "trace" is the framework of your lace; it's the fixing thread for all subsequent stitching. It is made by covering all the pattern's outlines with a double thread, the same as the thread you will be using for the lace, and held in place by fine thread. Only this tacking thread goes through the support "astride" the two cordonnet threads.

Doing the cordonnet properly is a very important step, because the quality of the finished work depends on it: it should therefore be firmly fixed to the support and sufficiently tight.

Cordonnet Thread

Before starting, you should make sure that your cordonnet thread is long enough to do the frame in one single operation.

SIMPLE CORDONNET

Here's how to make the cordonnet of a rectangle that has been pricked beforehand:

1. Measure the rectangle's perimeter and double the result to get the right length of cordonnet thread (blue in the photos).

2. Prepare a needle with tacking thread and pass it through one of the corners of the rectangle, from the reverse side to the right side, taking care to do a few anchoring stitches on the back of the cloth first.

Pass the needle through the loop of the doubled-over cordonnet thread (fig. 1). Return the needle to the original hole and pass it from the right side to the reverse side; the two threads (cordonnet and tacking) are now joined to the cloth (figs. 2 and 3).

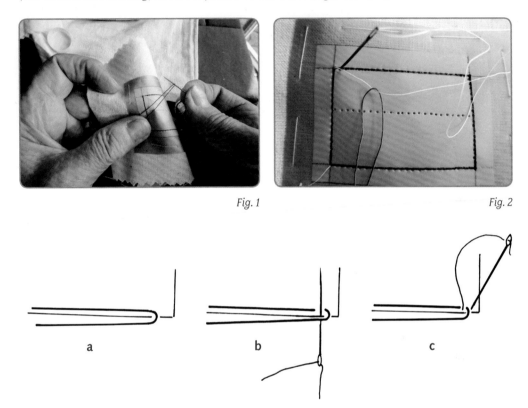

Fig. 1

Fig. 2

a

b

c

Fig. 3. Cordonnet thread and tacking thread
seen from above

3. Pass the needle through the next hole (2 mm apart), from the reverse side to the right side, pass the tacking thread over the two cordonnet threads, and return the needle to the hole it came out of, from the right side to the reverse side. Continue in the same way all around the outline of the rectangle. The cordonnet threads never go through the cloth; they lie on it and are held in place by the tacking thread, which goes in and out of the same pricked hole (fig. 4).

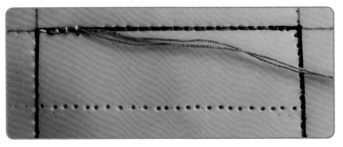

Fig. 4

4. To finish off and close the pattern's contour, using a crochet hook, crochet one of the cordonnet threads in the starting loop, then cross and separate the two threads. Do two more forward and two reverse stitches with the tacking thread, overlapping the others (fig. 5). Fix the tacking thread, using a few stitches on the reverse side of the cloth. Avoid knotting, which creates a thickness that will interfere with the rest of the work.

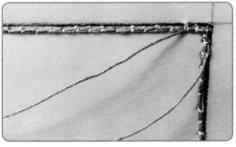

Fig. 5

Thimble

You can use a thimble to help you while making the cordonnet, but it is the only step in your work where it is allowed.

Cordonnet and fillings

Starting the ground (on the left)

WHEN THE CORDONNET HAS TO BRANCH OFF AND COME BACK

The cordonnet is usually done in a single operation, but sometimes the cordonnet has to branch off and then continue its progression. To avoid superposition, you should proceed like this:

1. Do the cordonnet normally until you reach the place where you need to branch off. You will use one of the two threads to do this.

2. Take the working thread to the farthest point of the line; using a couple of tacking stitches to keep it in place, hook it under the cordonnet of the leaf (fig. 1.)

3. Return normally, using the two threads that have now been made.

4. Take up your work with the two initial cordonnet threads (fig. 2.)

Fig. 1

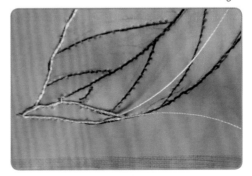

Fig. 2

Maintaining Your Work

There are two ways of doing needle lace: with or without a support.

Italian lacemakers use a tombolo, a small cushion on which are placed the pattern covered by transparent plastic, a sheet of paper, and a piece of cloth. Both hands are therefore free.

In France and in Flanders, lacemakers hold their work in their hands.

Lacemaker in Burano

Lacemakers in Alençon

In contrast to embroidery work, Alençon lacemakers work with the needle pointed upward. The needle is held in the right hand between the index finger and the middle finger (like a cigarette); the thumb holds the eye in place (figs. 1 and 2).

The correct position is important for the quality of the work. If it isn't followed, the results won't be good: the thread tension will be bad and the stitches irregular.

The thread, measured from your elbow to your fingertips, isn't pulled into the air but is held tight in front of you; it should slide along the work (figs. 3 and 4).

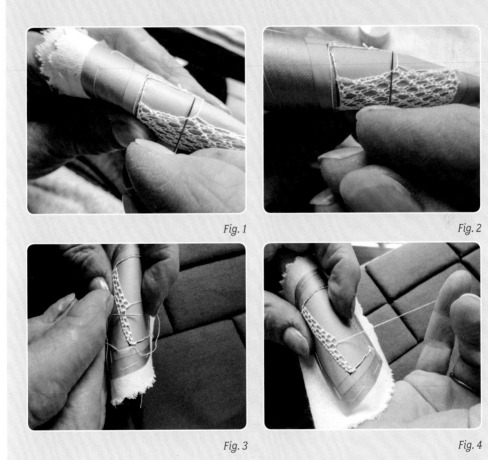

Fig. 1

Fig. 2

Fig. 3

Fig. 4

STARTING AND FINISHING THE FILLINGS

The fillings, which give the lace its opaque aspect, are made up of different stitches, which are detailed in the next chapter.

Here is how to start them (the example here is in tight Point de Gaze):

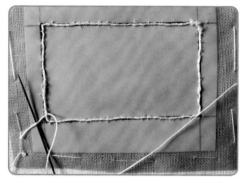

Fig. 1

Fig. 2

Fig. 3

1. Pass the needle with your working thread under the cordonnet from left to right, then go back and stitch through the working thread to block it (fig. 1).

2. Work using the buttonhole stitch (fig. 2) to the end of the first row. Attach the working thread to the cordonnet by passing over it and then under it (fig. 3). Work the thread from right to left (fig. 4). Start again by winding the working thread twice around the cordonnet, passing over it each time, and continue the buttonhole stitch.

Fixing the Thread

To stop the working thread coming free from your needle, you can make a small knot at the top of the needle's eye.

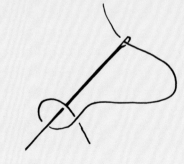

3. If you have to change the thread, do it at the end of a row. Pass the working thread under the cordonnet and stitch through the new thread as shown in fig. 1. Start again by passing under the cordonnet.

4. Finish the lace with a row of buttonhole stitch. If you don't have enough room to do another row, overcast the working thread to the cordonnet.

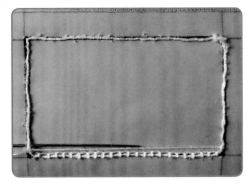

Fig. 4

Flat Knot

In needle lace, you should avoid making knots as often as possible, since these are a point of fragility.

However, sometimes it's unavoidable, such as when the working thread is too short or if it breaks a long way from the border. In this case you should do a flat knot and cut the two loose ends as close to the knot as possible.

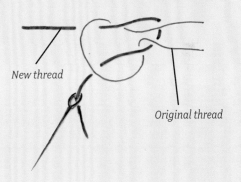

New thread

Original thread

SEPARATING, TRIMMING, SMOOTHING

These last steps in lacework, which are carried out once the top stitching is done, consist of separating the lace from its support and cleaning it. It is a delicate operation that needs a lot of care: it would be a real shame to spoil a piece of work that took so long to make!

1. Once the lace is finished, cut the tacking stitches that fixed the plastic to the cloth and open the two layers of cloth (fig. 1).

2. Using a razor blade, cut the tacking stitches that held the cordonnet in place (fig. 2). The lace will separate itself from its support (fig. 3).

3. Then we'll move on to trimming, which consists of using tweezers to remove all the little bits of loose thread on the underside of the lace (figs. 4 and 5).

4. "Polish" the fillings with a lobster's claw to accentuate the embroidery's relief: this step, called smoothing, can also be done with a cold iron. At the end of this step, all the little meshes in the lace will be correctly aligned side by side.

Fig. 1

Fig. 2

Fig. 3

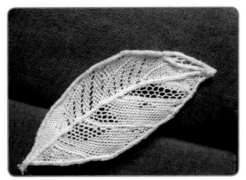

Fig. 4   Fig. 5

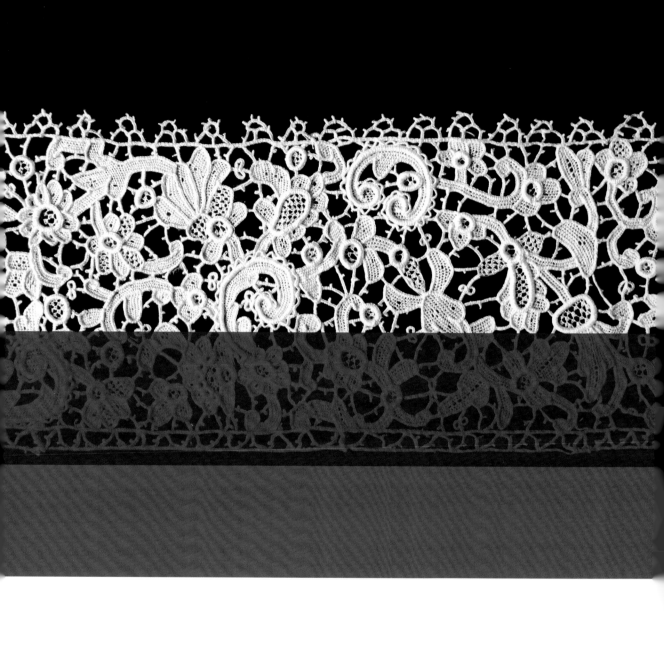

Principal Points
(Stitches)

In this chapter you will find the principal points used in needle lace, each explained step by step.

THESE POINTS ARE REGROUPED ACCORDING TO THEIR TYPE:

Fillings: Used to create the décor in lace, the fillings create shadowy effects.

❧

Top stitching: Composed of several thicker threads added in blanket stitch, it adds relief to the contours of the lace and consolidates it.

❧

Buttonhole stitch and its numerous variants: Ancestor of nets, it is also a fundamental element in needle lace.

❧

The ground: This serves as a background for the exterior parts of the pattern. Brides can replace it to join the patterns together (the brides are therefore regrouped into this category).

❧

Modes: These are the fancy, ornamental motifs as opposed to ground or fillings.

Embroidery

Mode

Filling

Ground

Types of lace stitches

Fillings

Different lacework, Alençon or Venetian for example, has its own names, knowledge, and particular points. Here we are using Brussels fillings. They are created from a sequence of buttonhole stitches.

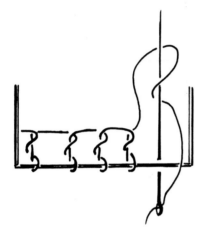

Alençon filling (twisted stitch)

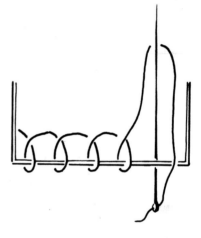

Brussels filling (buttonhole stitch)

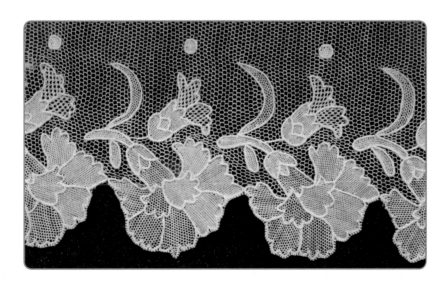

CLOSE POINT DE GAZE

Close gaze is the basic point, which gives more opaque results. Therefore it is one of the most widely used fillings.

HOW TO DO IT

The work uses buttonhole stitch (also called "loop stitch"), done one next to the other. To get a loop you must do two buttonhole stitches.

1. **1st row:** From left to right (each odd-numbered row is worked from left to right), do a row of buttonhole stitches and attach it to the cordonnet (see fig. 1 on page 40).

2. **2nd row:** For the second row, pull the thread from right to left (each even-numbered row is worked from right to left). Attach it to the cordonnet by winding the working thread twice round it, each time passing over the cordonnet (fig. 1). This creates a "cord."

3. **3rd row:** Do buttonhole stitches like the first row, each time taking up a loop from the first row and the cord from the second row (fig. 2).

4. **4th row:** The same as the second.

5. **Last row:** Finish the work with a row of buttonhole stitches. If you don't have room for this, fix the thread to the upper cordonnet with an overcast stitch.

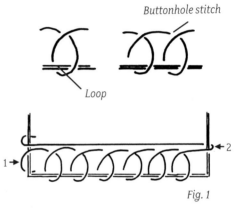

Buttonhole stitch

Loop

Fig. 1

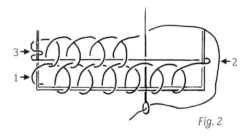

Fig. 2

Number of Loops

Generally, the number of loops should be the same from one row to another. But when making the interior of a motif whose contours are irregular, you should decrease or increase the number of loops accordingly at the beginning or at the end of the row.

WIDE POINT DE GAZE

In wide gaze, the space between the stitches is bigger than in close gaze, which makes it translucent. It is halfway between the fillings and the ground, which is transparent. It's a light stitch, but easily deformed; it is used alternately with close gaze to lighten the filled-in parts of the pattern.

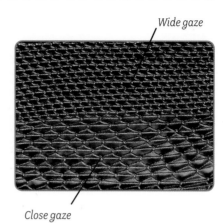

Wide gaze

Close gaze

HOW TO DO IT

1. 1st row: From left to right (odd-numbered rows), do a buttonhole stitch and then leave a space. Continue alternating buttonhole stitches and spaces to the end of the row. Your spaces and stitches should be identical in size and regular. Attach the thread to the cordonnet (see the figure on the right and page 40).

2. 2nd row: Pull the thread from right to left (even-numbered row) and attach it to the cordonnet to create a cord.

3. 3rd row: Do a buttonhole stitch, taking up both the thread from the 2nd row and the loop from the 1st row. Continue, respecting the alternating-space stitch.

4. Finish the wide gaze by a row of buttonhole stitches.

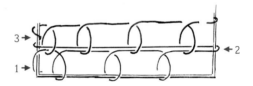

Top Stitching

Top stitching is done using close blanket stitch, which covers the cordonnet and the attaching stitches to give more relief to the contour of the pattern.

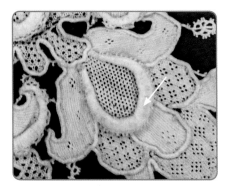

Top stitching can be emphasized by adding filler yarn, as in the Point de Venise, used since the seventeenth century.

HOW TO DO IT

Top stitching is always done toward the exterior. Four threads and horsehair, the length of the line to be covered, are used as filler yarn.

1. Lay down the filler yarn along the cordonnet, keeping the end in place with your left thumb. If they get in the way, wind a bit around a piece of cardboard.

2. After fixing your thread at the beginning the same way as for the other stitches (see page 40), do your blanket stitches, fixing them to the cordonnet. The blanket stitch should imprison the filler yarn and shouldn't overlap each other (fig. 1).

3. To finish off, slip the needle through the last two loops and cut the thread. Pull the filler yarn tight and cut it close to the cordonnet (fig. 2).

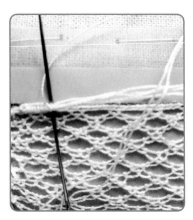

Fig. 1

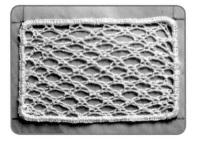

Fig. 2

Changing the Top Stitching Thread

If you have a lot of top stitching to do, one needleful of thread won't be enough. Proceed as follows to change the thread (this method can be used in a pinch during close gaze work, attaching it to a loop if the cordonnet is too far away, when doing a circle, for example):

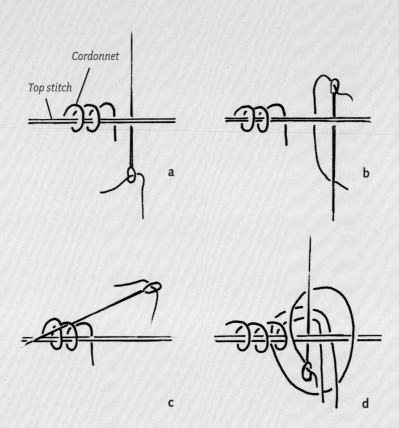

1. Pass the thread you are changing under the cordonnet from top to bottom. Introduce the new thread from bottom to top, close to the old one (a).

2. Stitch through the new thread to block it (b).

3. Return to your work, introducing the needle into the second-to-last loop (c).

4. Continue your blanket stitch, imprisoning the two working threads (d).

5. After two blanket stitches cut the end of the old thread, and after another two stitches, cut the end of the new thread.

TOP STITCHES WITH PICOTS

You can decorate your top stitches with picots, a sort of little teeth that adorn the edge of the lace. To make them, we use a pin as a support.

HOW TO DO IT

1. Start by doing a few blanket stitches as in a simple top stitch until you get to where the first picot will be added.

2. Form a loop by passing the thread behind the pin (it is used to maintain the loop). Pass the needle behind the loop and into the large loop formed by the thread to knot the picot in place (figs. 1 and 2). Don't remove the pin straight away.

3. Continue your work, adding picot in evenly spaced places (fig. 3).

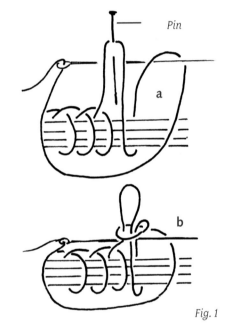

Fig. 1

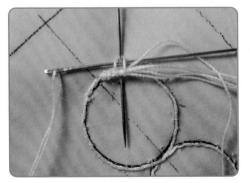

Fig. 2

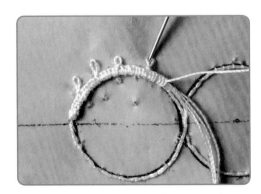

Fig. 3

ORNAMENTAL TOP STITCH

The top stitch can be worked in a decorative manner. For this we can add simple waves (along the bottom edge of the band), or overlapping waves (along the top of the band). These waves can be done one after the other or spaced apart.

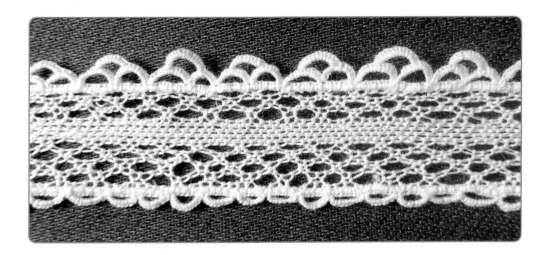

MAKING SIMPLE WAVES

1. Work with a fine needle. Prepare your support by marking the places where the waves will be, according to the size you want them to have.

2. To shape the first wave, do the top stitch according to the desired length for each wave (fig. 1).

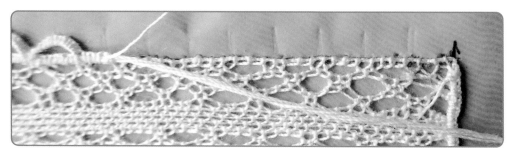

Fig. 1

3. Pull the thread toward the left, making a loop above the top stitch. Return to the beginning of the loop to create a wave with three threads (figs. 2 and 3). Attach the thread to the top stitch at each pass.

4. Do the top stitch with these three threads (figs. 4 and 5). You have just made your first wave. Continue the top stitch and repeat the steps.

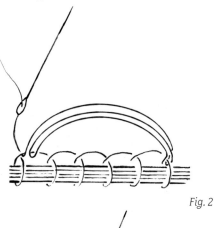

Fig. 2

Fig. 3

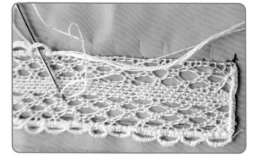

Fig. 4

Fig. 5

MAKING TRIPLE WAVES

1. Do two waves, side by side, in the same way as simple waves, but topstitch only half of the second wave. Stop there (fig. 6).

2. Pull the three threads to form a third wave (fig. 7).

3. Once the third wave is finished, continue the top stitch on the second wave (figs. 8 and 9).

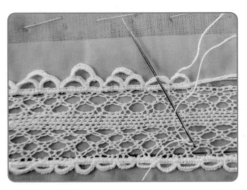

Fig. 6

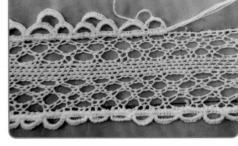

Fig. 7

Fig. 8

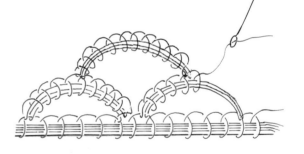

Fig. 9

Buttonhole Stitch with a Cord

The richness of needle lace lies in the great number of variants of the decorative and filling points. To start off, here are the principal points worked in buttonhole stitch, with a cord after each row of buttonhole stitch.

Fixing to the Cordonnet

For all buttonhole stitches with a cord, keep in mind that we attach the thread once to the cordonnet for the rows from left to right (before making the cord) and twice after the rows from right to left (before doing a new row of loops).

VARIANT 1

HOW TO DO IT

1. 1st row: from left to right (odd-numbered rows), do two buttonhole stitches and then leave a space the size of two buttonhole stitches. Continue to alternate two stitches with two spaces to the end of the row and attach the thread to the cordonnet.

2. 2nd row: Pull the thread from right to left (even-numbered rows) and attach it to the cordonnet at the end of the row.

3. 3rd row: Skip the first two loops. Do two buttonhole stitches over the spaces in row one, taking up the thread of the latter and the cord. Continue and attach the thread to the cordonnet at the end of the row.

4. 4th row: The same as the 2nd row.

5. Repeat the rows as often as necessary.

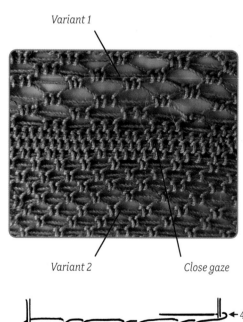

Variant 1

Variant 2　　　　　Close gaze

56

VARIANT 2
HOW TO DO IT

1. **1st row:** From left to right (odd-numbered rows), do three buttonhole stitches, then leave a space the size of three stitches. Continue to alternate three stitches with a space to the end of the row and attach the thread to the cordonnet.

2. **2nd row:** Pull the thread from right to left to make a cord (even-numbered rows) and attach it to the cordonnet at the end of the row.

3. **3rd row:** Skip the first two stitches. Do three buttonhole stitches over the space in row one, taking up the thread of the latter and the cord. Continue and attach the thread to the cordonnet at the end of the row.

4. **4th row:** the same as the second row.

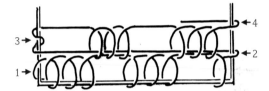

VARIANT 3

This variant allows you to make the point thicker and accentuate certain motifs such as the veins in a leaf. The stitch is worked with several threads on the cord. The amount depends on the desired effect, but they are always odd numbered to respect the direction of the work.

HOW TO DO IT

1. **1st row (odd-numbered rows):** Work the buttonhole stitches from left to right.

2. **2nd row (even-numbered rows):** Pull as many threads as necessary from right to left to create a thick cord (in the diagram opposite, we have used five threads).

3. **3rd row:** Continue the buttonhole stitches, taking up each loop in the 1st row and the threads of the cord in the 2nd row.

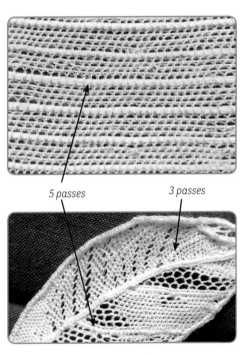

5 passes   *3 passes*

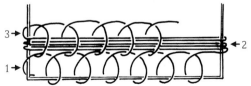

VARIANT 4

This point creates lines in relief. According to the direction of the work, it can make horizontal or vertical lines that adapt to the work.

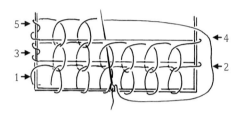

HOW TO DO IT

1. 1st row (odd-numbered rows): Do a first row of buttonhole stitches from left to right.

2. 2nd row (even-numbered rows): Pull the thread from right to left and attach it to the cordonnet.

3. 3rd row: Do a row of buttonhole stitches, taking up the loop in the 1st row and the cord in the 2nd.

4. 4th row: The same as the 2nd.

VARIANT 5 (Diagonal Holes)

HOW TO DO IT

1. 1st row (odd-numbered rows): Do a row of buttonhole stitches from left to right.

2. Choose the number of holes and the rate of their repetitions in the row. Displace them the same number of stitches as you proceed to create diagonals.

3. 2nd row (even-numbered rows): Pull the thread from right to left and overcast each of the loops that will be used to form the diagonal holes.

4. 3rd row: Do a row of buttonhole stitches. Skip the overcast loop and continue the stitches to the next hole.

5. 4th row: Pull the thread, overcasting the loop preceding the hole in the row below as well as this loop.

6. 5th row: Do two buttonhole stitches in the hole and go on to the following loop.

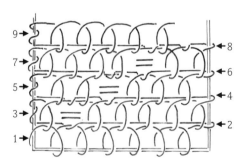

VARIANT 6
(Diamond or Fly)

This point consists of making holes in close gaze. These holes can be isolated or spread out over several rows, to create a motif.

HOW TO DO IT

1. 1st row: (odd-numbered rows): Do a row of close gaze from left to right.

2. 2nd row: (even-numbered rows): Pull the thread from right to left to the place where the first fly will be. Overcast the loop in the lower row once and pull the thread to the following fly (fig. 1).

3. 3rd row: Do your close gaze to the overcast loop. Skip it and then do a twisted stitch (see page 47) in the following loop (fig. 2).

4. 4th row: Pull the thread. Overcast once in the loop preceding the twisted stitch, twice in the hole, and once in the flowing loop (fig. 3).

5. 5th row: Do your stitches to the first overcast loop. Skip the two overcast loops and do a twisted stitch in the hole. Skip the following overcast loops and then do a twisted stitch in the following loop (fig. 3).

6. 6th row: Pull the thread and overcast twice each of the two openings (fig. 3).

7. 7th row: Work up to the first opening. Do two buttonhole stitches in it and then a twisted stitch and a buttonhole stitch in the second opening (fig. 4).

8. 8th row: Pull the thread and overcast twice in the last opening (fig. 4).

9. 9th row: Continue in close gaze as in the 1st row and continue the following rows as often as necessary (fig. 4).

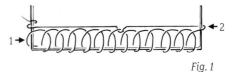

Fig. 1

Fig. 2

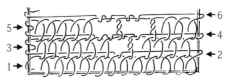

Fig. 3

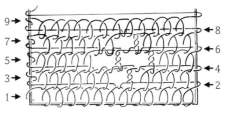

Fig. 4

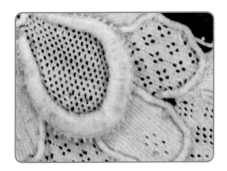

VARIANT 7 (Zigzag)

In early lace work, zigzags were used as fillings for small areas, such as the heart of a flower.

The zigzag point has two forms; when using the second method you will get larger openings.

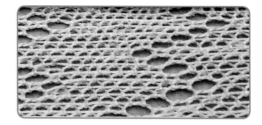

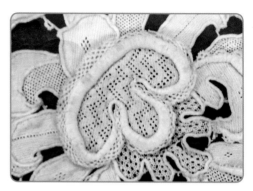

HOW TO DO IT (Method 1)

1. 1st row (odd-numbered rows): From left to right, start by leaving a space and then continue the row with buttonhole stitches.

2. Choose the place where the zigzags will be and the rate of their repetitions in the row.

3. 2nd row (even-numbered rows): Pull the thread from right to left and overcast each of the loops that will be used to form the zigzags.

4. 3rd row: Do your buttonhole stitches up to the first overcast loop. Skip it and continue to the next overcast loop. Continue in the same way to the end of the row.

5. 4th row: Pull the thread from right to left, overcasting twice in the spaces and once in the loop after each space (you are thereby displacing the openings toward the left from row to row). Continue to the end of the row.

6. 5th row: Skip the overcast loop in the row below and do two buttonhole stitches in each opening; continue to the next overcast loop. Continue to the end of the row (fig. 1).

7. Continue in the same way to the 5th row of holes, then start displacing the holes toward the right, by overcasting once in the preceding space and twice in the space (fig. 3).

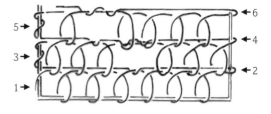

Fig. 1

HOW TO DO IT (Method 2)

Another method consists of doing a twisted stitch (see page 47) after each space (fig. 2), the same as in the diamond (page 59).

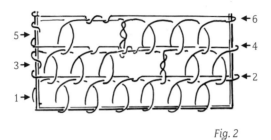

Fig. 2

Fig. 3: Zigzag point (the cords aren't shown, to make understanding it easier). The red line shows the place where the spaces are.

VARIANT 8 (Quadrille)

Quadrille gaze is done in buttonhole stitch. To shape the small lozenges, you must make sure you have the same number of stitches on each side.

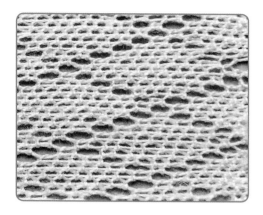

HOW TO DO IT

1. 1st row (odd-numbered rows): Working from left to right, leave a space at the beginning of the row and then do as many buttonhole stitches as you want (they will determine the length of the lozenge). Leave a new space and then do the same number of buttonhole stitches as before. Continue to the end of the row.

2. 2nd row (even-numbered rows): Pull the thread from right to left, overcasting the first space and the loop after it. Pull the thread to the loop before the next space; overcast it and also the space after it. Continue in the same way to the end of the row.

3. 3rd row: Do two buttonhole stitches over the first space. Skip the overcast loop; continue to the next overcast loop and skip it. Do two buttonhole stitches over the space after it. Continue to the end of the row.

4. 4th–9th rows: Alternate rows 2 and 3.

5. 10th row: Pull the thread, overcasting the loop before the last space, and the space and the loop after it, to restart on each side (fig. 1).

6. Continue in the same way until the spaces rejoin each other. Overcast the loop before the space, and the space and the loop after it, and then restart in the opposite direction on each side (fig. 2). Be careful to count the stitches to make sure you have the same number on each side.

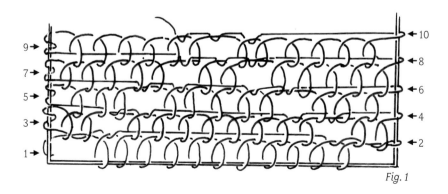

Fig. 1

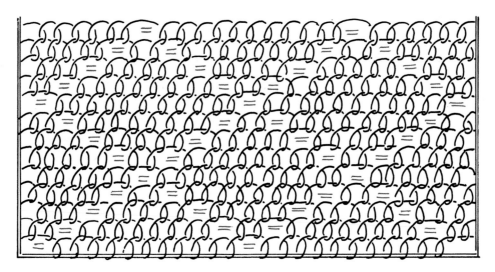

Fig. 2: The quadrille (the cords aren't shown, to make understanding it easier). The red line shows the place where the spaces are.

VARIANT 9 (Buttonhole)

This variant is so-named because it creates an aspect similar to buttonholes. It gives a pretty effect to your lace.

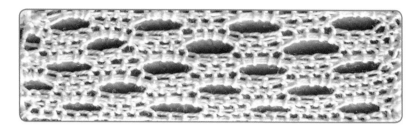

HOW TO DO IT

1. 1st row (odd-numbered rows): Do a row of buttonhole stitches and attach the thread to the cordonnet.

2. 2nd row (even-numbered rows): Pull the thread from right to left.

3. 3rd row: Do four buttonhole stitches, skip three loops, and do four more buttonhole stitches. Continue in the same way to the end of the row.

4. 4th row: The same as the 2nd row.

5. 5th row: Start your buttonhole stitches. Do four stitches over each space in the lower row, taking up the three threads in the lower rows.

6. 6th row: The same as the 2nd row.

7. 7th row: The same as the 1st row.

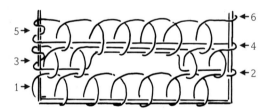

Buttonhole Stitch without a Cord

For all the following points that don't use a cord on each even-numbered row, you should attach the thread to the cordonnet twice at the beginning and at the end of each row.

Direction of the work

The direction of the thread changes between the odd-numbered and even-numbered rows: whether working from right to left or left to right, the buttonhole stitches should follow the same direction, as shown below.

VARIANT 1
HOW TO DO IT

1. 1st row (odd-numbered rows): Working from left to right, do a row of buttonhole stitches and attach the thread to the cordonnet at the end of the row.

2. 2nd row (even-numbered rows): Before starting, attach the thread to the cordonnet again and do a row of buttonhole stitches from right to left and attach the thread to the cordonnet at the end of the row.

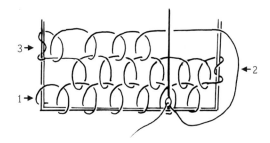

3. 3rd row: Attach the thread to the cordonnet again and continue as the first row. Continue for as many rows as necessary.

VARIANT 2
HOW TO DO IT

1. 1st row: Do this row alternating two buttonhole stitches and one space. Finish the row and attach the thread to the cordonnet.

2. 2nd row: Attach the thread to the cordonnet. Do two buttonhole stitches over the space. Skip the next loop and do two more buttonhole stitches over the following space. Continue the row in this way. Finish the row and attach the thread to the cordonnet.

3. Continue, alternating the two rows as often as necessary.

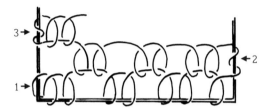

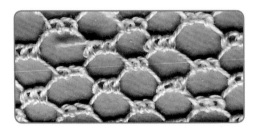

VARIANT 3
HOW TO DO IT

1. 1st row: Alternate three buttonhole stitches and one space to the end of the row and attach the thread to the cordonnet.

2. 2nd row: Attach the thread to the cordonnet again and work from right to left, doing three buttonhole stitches over the space. Skip the next two buttonhole stitches and do three over the following space. Continue in this way to the end of the row and attach the thread to the cordonnet.

3. Alternate these rows as often as necessary.

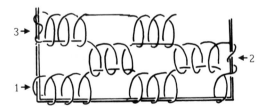

VARIANT 4
HOW TO DO IT

1. 1st row: Alternate three buttonhole stitches and one space to the end of the row. Attach the thread to the cordonnet.

2. 2nd row: Attach the thread to the cordonnet again and work from right to left, doing a buttonhole stitch over the lower space. Skip the next two loops and do a buttonhole stitch over the next space. Continue in this way to the end of the row and attach the thread to the cordonnet.

3. Alternate these two rows to the end of your piece of work.

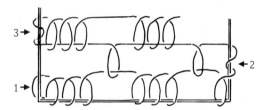

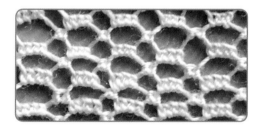

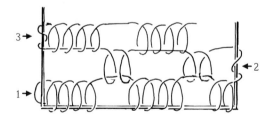

VARIANT 5
HOW TO DO IT

1. 1st row: Do four buttonhole stitches and then leave a space, until the end of the row. Attach the thread to the cordonnet.

2. 2nd row: Attach the thread to the cordonnet again and work from right to left, doing two buttonhole stitches over the space, and then skip the three loops after it. Continue this way to the end of the row. Attach the thread to the cordonnet.

3. Continue, alternating these two rows as often as necessary.

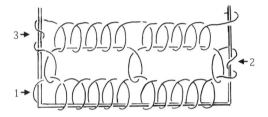

VARIANT 6
HOW TO DO IT

1. 1st row: Make five buttonhole stitches and then leave a space. Continue in this way to the end of the row and attach the thread to the cordonnet.

2. 2nd row: Attach the thread to the cordonnet again and work from right to left, doing one buttonhole stitch over the space in the lower row. Skip the four loops after it and do a buttonhole stitch over the next space. Continue in this way to the end of the row and attach the thread to the cordonnet.

3. 3rd row: The same as the 1st row.

VARIANT 7
(Point de Brabant)

Besides Brussels lace, which is very fine and expensive, there is another lace, a little coarser with a less refined ground, called "Brabant lace" (or "Flanders lace"). This point obviously got its name from this type of lace.

HOW TO DO IT

1. 1st row: Make a buttonhole stitch and then leave a space; then a buttonhole stitch and leave three spaces. Continue in this way to the end of the row.

2. 2nd row: Working from right to left, make three buttonhole stitches over the three-hole space below, leave a space, and then do a buttonhole stitch over the loop and another three buttonhole stitches over the next three-hole space. Continue in this way to the end of the row.

3. 3rd row: The same as the 1st row.

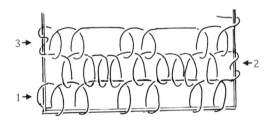

VARIANT 8 (Point Flamand)

If bobbin lace was popular in Flanders, needle lace wasn't neglected and the former gave inspiration to the latter.

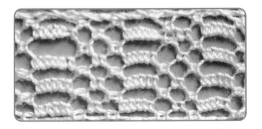

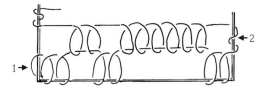

HOW TO DO IT

1. **1st row:** Do two buttonhole stitches and leave a space; do two more stitches and leave six spaces. Continue in this way and attach the thread to the cordonnet at the end of the row.

2. **2nd row:** Attach the thread to the cordonnet again; working from right to left, skip the first loop. Do six buttonhole stitches over the space in the lower row. Skip the next loop and do two buttonhole stitches. Skip the next loop and continue in the same way.

3. **3rd row:** The same as the 1st row.

VARIANT 9 (Simple Pea or Open Spider)
HOW TO DO IT

1. 1st row: Do a row of buttonhole stitches.

2. 2nd row: Do two buttonhole stitches and then skip two loops and so on to the end of the row (fig. 1).

3. 3rd row: Do a complete row of buttonhole stitches, doing three buttonhole stitches over the spaces in the lower row and one in the one in the single loop (fig. 2).

4. 4th row: The same as the 2nd row.

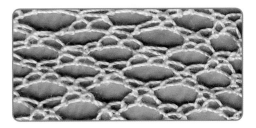

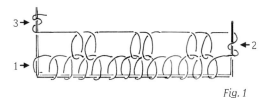

Fig. 1

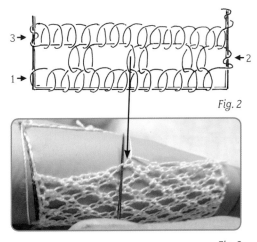

Fig. 2

Fig. 3

VARIANT 10 (Point de Bruxelles)

This very open point is typical of Brussels lace and is named after it.

1. 1st row: Make a row of buttonhole stitches.

2. 2nd row: Do a buttonhole stitch, skip three loops, and do a buttonhole stitch. Continue in the same way to the end of the row.

3. 3rd row: Make four buttonhole stitches over the large space. Leave a space and do four more buttonhole stitches. Continue in the same way to the end of the row.

4. 4th row: Make a buttonhole stitch over the middle of the group of four stitches. Skip three loops and do another buttonhole stitch.

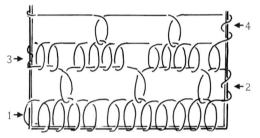

VARIANT 11 (Half Pyramid)
HOW TO DO IT

1. 1st row: Do the row alternating four buttonhole stitches and a space.

2. 2nd row: Make three buttonhole stitches and then leave a space. Continue in this way, alternating three buttonhole stitches and a space.

3. 3rd row: Skip two loops. Do four buttonhole stitches over the space in the lower row. Continue in this way: a space of two loops and then four buttonhole stitches.

4. 4th row: Skip the space, do three buttonhole stitches over the three loops, then skip the space after. Continue in this way to the end of the row.

5. 5th row: The same as the 1st row. Do the four buttonhole stitches over the spaces and skip the two loops to create new spaces.

6. Continue as long as necessary, repeating these 5 rows.

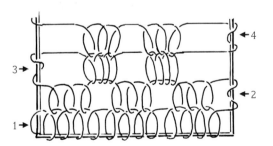

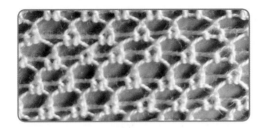

VARIANT 12
HOW TO DO IT

1. 1st row: Make a row of buttonhole stitches.

2. 2nd row: Make a buttonhole stitch over every second loop.

3. 3rd row: Make two buttonhole stitches over the spaces.

4. 4th row: The same as the 2nd row.

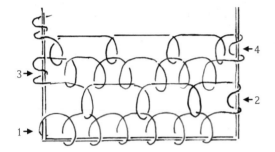

VARIANT 13 (Small Pyramid)

Pyramids are triangular shaped and create very pretty effects. They can be different sizes.

HOW TO DO IT

1. 1st row: Work this row alternating three buttonhole stitches and a space.

2. 2nd row: Leave a space. Do a buttonhole stitch over each loop in the row below and leave a space. Continue in this way to the end of the row.

3. 3rd row: Leave a space and do a buttonhole stitch over every loop in the lower row, but not over the spaces.

4. 4th row: The same as the first row, but working from right to left (even-numbered row).

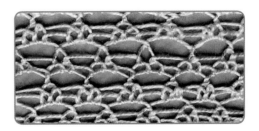

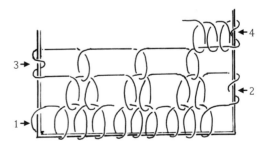

VARIANT 14 (Large Pyramid)
HOW TO DO IT

1. 1st row: Alternate five buttonhole stitches and a space throughout the row.

2. 2nd row: Make a buttonhole stitch over each of the four loops in the lower row and skip the space. Continue in this way to the end of the row.

3. 3rd row: Alternate three buttonhole stitches and a space.

4. 4th row: Alternate two buttonhole stitches and a space.

5. 5th row: Make one buttonhole stitch and leave a large space.

6. 6th row: The same as the first row. Do five buttonhole stitches and skip the loop.

7. 7th row: Continue the 6 rows as often as necessary.

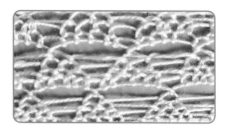

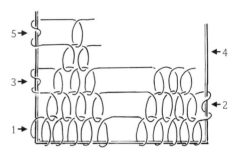

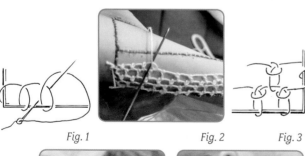

Fig. 1   Fig. 2   Fig. 3

Fig. 4   Fig. 5

VARIANT 15 (Point Venetian)

This point, created in Venice, is also called "cross stitch."

HOW TO DO IT

1. 1st row: Do a buttonhole stitch. To create the second, pass the needle through the loop you have just made (figs. 1 and 2), then leave a space. Continue in this way to the end of the row.

2. 2nd row: As in the first row, do a buttonhole stitch over the space, pass the needle through the newly made loop to make the second stitch (figs. 3 to 5) and then leave a space. Continue in this way to the end of the row.

3. 3rd row: The same as the 1st row.

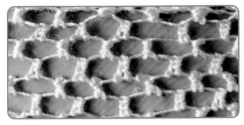

VARIANT 16 (Double Loop)
HOW TO DO IT

1. 1st row: Make two buttonhole stitches close together. Pass the needle through the first loop (the first corresponds to the space formed between the cordonnet and the first buttonhole stitch), turn the working thread from right to left, and do two buttonhole stitches following fig. 1. Do two more buttonhole stitches and continue in the same way.

2. 2nd row: Working from right to left, do two buttonhole stitches, pass the needle through the first loop twice, and continue in this way to the end of the row (fig. 2).

3. Repeat these rows as often as necessary (figs. 3 and 4).

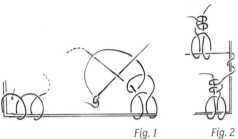

Fig. 1   *Fig. 2*

Fig. 3. Working from left to right

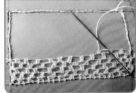

Fig. 4. Working from right to left

VARIANT 17 (Point de Venice or Point de Grain)
HOW TO DO IT

1. 1st row: Make a large buttonhole stitch and then do four buttonhole stitches in the loop (fig. 1). Continue in this way to the end of the row.

2. 2nd row: Working from right to left, do a large buttonhole stitch over the stitches in the lower row (fig. 2). To do this, overcast the large buttonhole stitch at the start. Be careful to keep these stitches apart from the Point de Venice since they will serve for the following point.

3. 3rd row: The same as the 1st row.

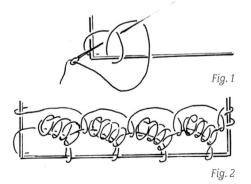

Fig. 1

Fig. 2

VARIANT 18

To obtain this variant, the needle doesn't pass through the loop but through the stitch. In this way the buttonhole stitches overlap one into the other without any gap.

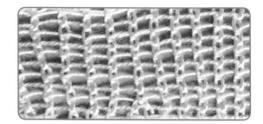

HOW TO DO IT

1. 1st row: Make a row of buttonhole stitches.

2. 2nd row: Make a loop with the thread to the left of the needle and pass it through the buttonhole stitch in the lower row to create the first stitch of the row. Continue in the same way to the end of the row.

3. 3rd row: The same as the 2nd row.

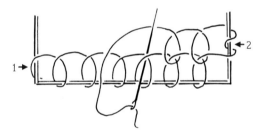

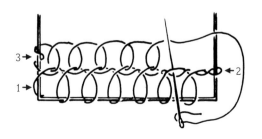

VARIANT 19
HOW TO DO IT

1. 1st row: Make a row of buttonhole stitches.

2. 2nd row: Working from right to left, overcast each loop.

3. 3rd row: Make a row of buttonhole stitches, passing the needle only through the overcast and the first loop at the start of the row.

4. Continue these three rows as often as necessary.

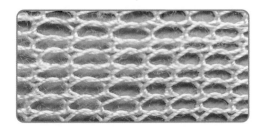

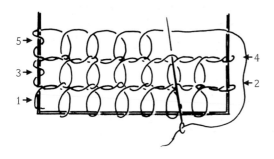

VARIANT 20
HOW TO DO IT

1. 1st row: Make a row of buttonhole stitches.

2. 2nd row: Working from right to left, overcast each loop.

3. 3rd row: Make a row of buttonhole stitches, passing the needle only through the overcast.

4. 4th row: The same as the 2nd row.

VARIANT 21
HOW TO DO IT

1. 1st row: Make a row of buttonhole stitches.

2. 2nd row: Working from right to left, overcast each loop.

3. 3rd row: Make a row of buttonhole stitches, passing the needle through the overcast in row 2 and the loops in row 1.

4. 4th row: The same as the 2nd row.

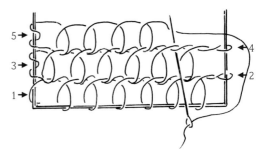

round

The ground, which serves as the background to the exterior parts of a pattern, is mainly made up of Point de Tulle and brides. Carried out using fine thread for better results, the Point de Tulle forms light grounds, which have replaced brides little by little. The Alençon Point de Tulle was one of the best known.

SIMPLE POINT DE TULLE
HOW TO DO IT

1. 1st row: Alternate a twisted stitch and a space to the end of the row.

2. 2nd row: From right to left, do twisted stitches.

3. Reproduce these rows as often as necessary.

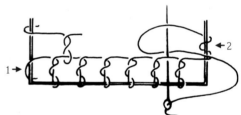

ALENÇON POINT DE TULLE

The Point d'Alençon is a complex variant of the Point de Tulle; it is done using twisted stitches; that is to say, wound round the needle (figs. 1 and 2). Each stitch is overcast three times to the following row. It is generally done with fine thread to highlight its lightness.

The biggest difficulty in its creation lies in the regularity of the loops. The location of the starting point on the cordonnet determines the height of the loops and the rows.

HOW TO DO IT

1. 1st row: Alternate a twisted stitch and a space to the end of the row (fig. 1).

2. 2nd row: From right to left, overcast each loop three times (fig. 2).

3. 3rd row: The same as the 1st row.

4. Finish by fastening each loop of the last row to the cordonnet with three stitches to maintain the space between the points. If you don't have enough room to do a row of stitches, overcast the thread to attach it to the cordonnet.

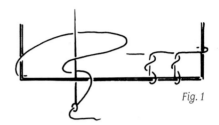

Fig. 1

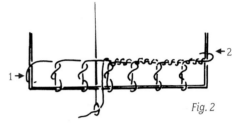

Fig. 2

BURANO POINT DE TULLE

This variant is the Point de Tulle overcast once.

HOW TO DO IT

Work in the same way as the Alençon Point de Tulle, but in the even-numbered rows, overcast the loops only once.

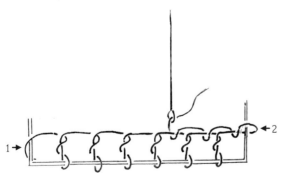

BRIDE

The bride, present in lacework since the Renaissance, is made up of three threads worked in blanket stitch, which are then used to join lace patterns together. They are also called "bars."

An area of more-important brides, organized in even hexagonal loops, differentiates the lace from the guipure.

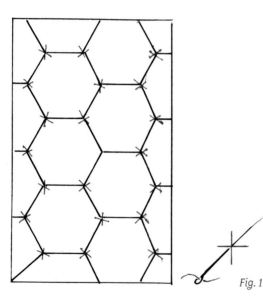

Fig. 1

HOW TO DO IT

1. Prepare a support for this sample the (one shown here measures 5 × 8 cm). Mark the location of the hexagons. To make the frame, mark the six tops of the hexagons with crosses of fine tacking thread (fig. 1). This stay stitching serves to tighten the three supporting threads.

Stay stitches

Stay stitches are used to direct the threads. They are done with a needleful of fine thread, and there are two sorts: running stitch and cross-stitch.

To do them, pass the needle through the two layers of cloth, the pattern, and the plastic. On your work, do either a running stitch or a cross-stitch according to the instructions. Do a few securing stitches on the back of the cloth. These threads will disappear when you remove the lace from its support.

2. Work from the bottom toward the top. Start on the left side as shown in fig. 2. With the thread, reproduce the line in zigzag following the arrows, by passing through each of the stay stitches. Work the horizontal lines at the same time by branching off. The horizontal line will now have a second thread (fig. 2.1). Continue the zigzags and horizontal lines to the top of the support. Fix the thread to the cordonnet.

Reminder

Keep in mind that the cordonnet has two threads, the bride has three, and the top stitch has four.

Follow the arrows: work from the bottom to the top on odd-numbered rows and from the top to the bottom on even-numbered rows.

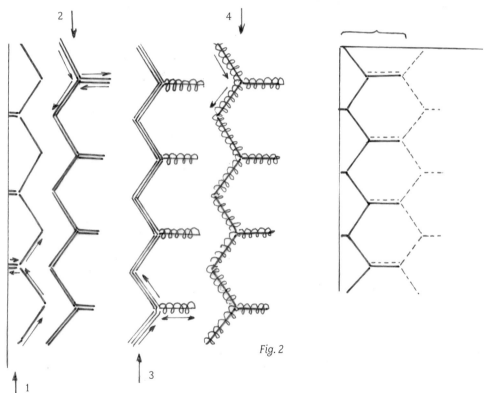

Fig. 2

3. Go down on the right with a second thread. Go through each stay stitch but don't pass over the horizontal lines (fig. 2.2).

4. In the same way, go back up on the left with a third thread without passing through the horizontal lines (fig. 2.3).

5. Come back down on the right, doing a buttonhole stitch. At each junction of the bride (called a bar), pull the thread on the horizontal lines to the following junction and come back doing buttonhole stitches (figs. 2.3 and 2.4). The horizontal lines, like the other lines, contain three threads (there were already two in the construction of the frame). It is important to always do the buttonhole stitches in the same direction so that they have the same orientation.

6. To finish, buttonhole-stitch the left side, working from bottom to top.

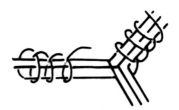

Fig. 3

Changing direction

When there is a change of direction, always pass the needle under the stitch so that the buttonhole stitch doesn't get twisted.

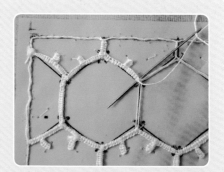

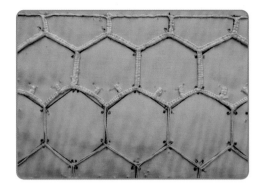

BRIDE WITH PICOTS

Picots are ornaments that embellish the bars of the bride. They are done using fine thread, making sure that they aren't too close to the bride so that the picots aren't too small (the farther apart the tacking thread, the larger the picot).

HOW TO DO IT

The picots are done at the same time as the bride.

1. Put in tacking stitches at the location of the picots (you can use a pin to mark the spot instead of tacking stitches), making sure they aren't too close to the hexagons.

2. Do your bride up to the location of the first picot (fig. 1).

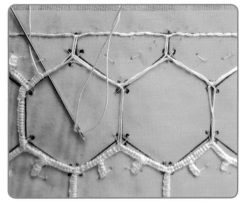

Fig. 1

3. Pass the needle under the three threads and into the tacking stitch. Repeat this twice to create a cord of three threads (figs. 2–4).

4. Turn the thread to change direction (see page 80). Start your buttonhole stitches on the cord until you reach the starting point, and then continue as before.

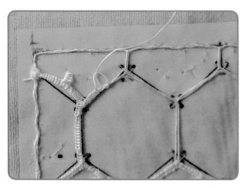

Fig. 2

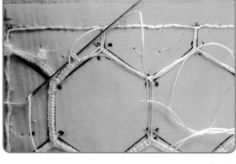

Fig. 3

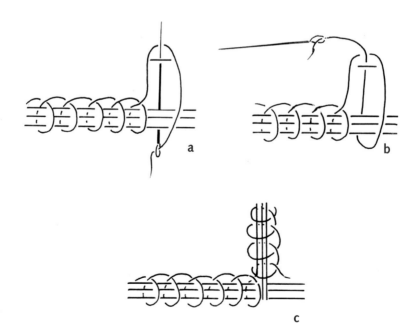

Fig. 4

DECORATED BRIDES

The brides shown here are intended for the ground; they are used in modern needle lace to fill small spaces. They are very decorative and can also be used as trimmings, for flower stalks that are too fine for fillings, for example, or to represent geometrical patterns.

Sometimes they are used to solidify a piece of work or to maintain small knots or pearls.

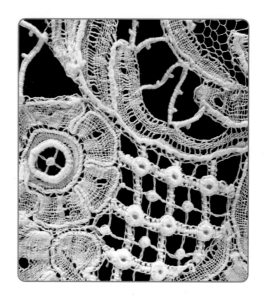

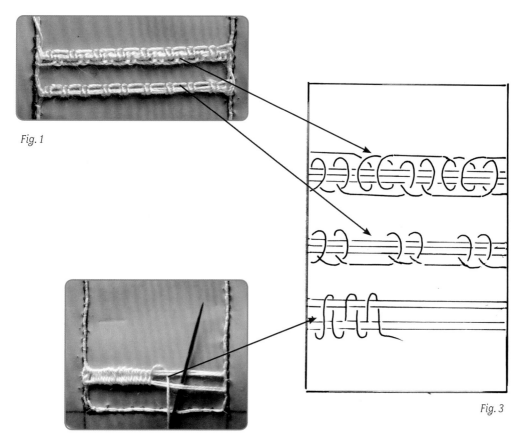

Fig. 1

Fig. 2

Fig. 3

Modes

Modes are ornamental jours (holes) in needle lace. To make them it's often necessary to use stay stitches with tacking thread that will serve as supports for the points.

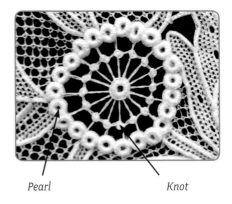

Pearl   *Knot*

SMALL KNOTS

Small knots are a recurring ornament in needle lace. They are used for the hearts of flowers, roses, or fillings; around a pearl; or along a line; for example.

HOW TO DO IT

1. With the same thread that you use for the rest of the piece of work, create a cord the height of the pattern to be covered, and fix it to the cordonnet and then oversew it from top to bottom (not buttonhole stitch) the length of the line. You can also make a double cord directly. Create another cord at a distance of 0.5 cm and so forth the length of the pattern (figs. 1 and 2).

2. Create a quadrille with horizontal threads and attach them to the cordonnet. Fix each junction with a vertical line with a backstitch (fig. 3).

   To make these intersections more solid, you can do stay stitches at the center of each intersection (see stay stitches on page 78).

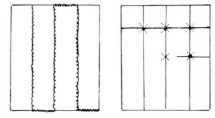

Fig. 1

Fig. 2

3. At the end of the first horizontal line, attach the thread to the cordonnet and work backward, overcasting to the first junction to create the first knot.

4. At the junction do three diagonal buttonhole stitches in the same direction (figs. 4a, 5a, and 6).

5. Do a diagonal buttonhole stitch in the opposite direction (figs. 4b and 5b).

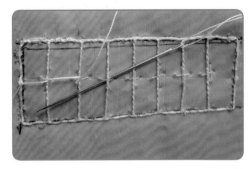

Fig. 3

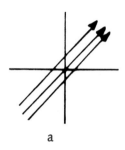
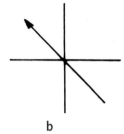
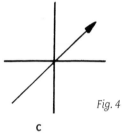

Fig. 4

a b c

6. Finally, do a buttonhole stitch in the first direction (figs. 4c and 5c).

7. Wind the thread round the knot that has just been made (fig. 7).

8. Overcast the horizontal thread to the second junction.

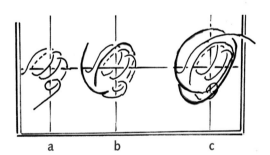

a b c

Fig. 5

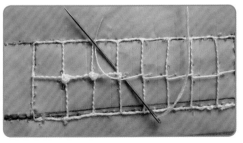

Fig. 6

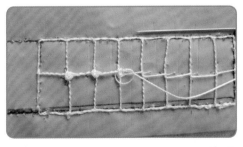

Fig. 7

POINT D'ESPIRT

Lace makers know the Point d'Esprit very well, such as those used in Cluny or Torchon bobbin lace and also in needle lace. It is a very decorative point that is done between two cordonnets.

HOW TO DO IT

1. Prepare two cordonnets, between which the Point d'Esprit will be fixed (fig. 1).

2. Do a row of wide-spaced (about 0.5 cm apart) buttonhole stitches along the two cordonnets, passing the thread in the cordonnet (fig. 2). Make sure that these large loops are in the same place on each cordonnet (fig. 2).

3. Start the Point d'Esprit by winding the thread once or twice round the first of the large loops. Pull the thread to the opposite loop and pass the needle through it and then return to the first loop. Repeat four or six times. The whole should be close together but flat (fig. 3).

4. Finish the Point d'Esprit on the same side you started. Wind the thread once around the loop to fix it.

5. Do the other loops in the same way.

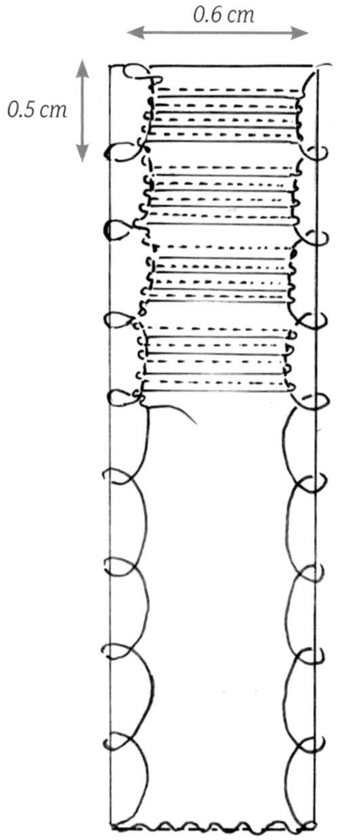

Fig. 1

Fig. 2

Fig. 3

STAR

Stars are needle lace ornaments used to embellish intersections. They are made up of picots.

HOW TO DO IT

1. Start by placing your stay stitches (see page 78) with a fine thread (fig. 1). Don't do these too close to the bride.

2. Pull three support threads horizontally from right to left, passing under the stay stitches.

3. Do a row of buttonhole stitches along the horizontal line, leaving a space where the horizontal and vertical lines will cross (fig. 2 and 3).

4. Pull three threads vertically and buttonhole-stitch them to the intersection.

5. Start the first picot by pulling three threads from the intersection to one of the stay stitches. Buttonhole stitch it to the center of the star (fig. 4).

6. Pass the thread behind and repeat the operation until you have three more picots (fig. 5).

7. Finish the row. When you start buttonhole-stitching the other brides, after doing the four picots, pull the first stitch toward the heart of the star.

Direction of your work

Make sure that you do your buttonhole stitches in the same direction so that their knots will always be in the same direction.

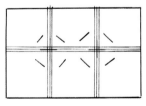

Fig. 1

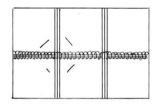

Fig. 2

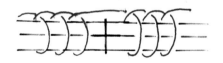

Fig. 3

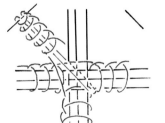

Fig. 4

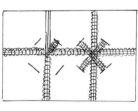

Fig. 5

PETALS

Here, each petal is done independently.

HOW TO DO IT

1. Prepare your support (the one shown here measures 4 × 6 cm). Make a rectangle with two horizontal lines and three vertical lines.

2. With fine thread, put in your stay stitches (see page 78) in crosses at the places where the junctions will be (see the photo below).

3. Lay the three support threads along the horizontal and vertical lines and fix them to the cordonnet. Pass them under the stay stitches (fig. 1 of the preceding page).

4. Buttonhole stitch the vertical lines as a bride (see page 78), leaving a space where they cross the horizontal lines (figs. 2 and 3 of the preceding page).

5a. To make a simple petal, work on the horizontal bar up to the first stay stitch. Make a loop by passing the thread three times through the stay stitch and under the three threads of the bride (figs. 1 and 2). Topstitch the three loops all around the petal (figs. 3 and 4). Continue to the next petal.

Fig. 1

Fig. 2

Fig. 3

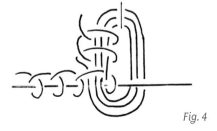

Fig. 4

5b. To make two petals, proceed as previously to make the first petal and in the other direction for the second petal. Continue to the next petal.

5c. To create four petals, lay three threads to form a cross to be able to do the petals in one go (fig. 5).
For this, pass the thread under the stay stitches and under the thread created by the horizontal and vertical brides (see step 4), following the direction shown in fig. 5. Renew the operation twice, to have three filler threads. After the last pass, topstitch the three threads all around their contours (fig. 6).

6. When you reach the place where the petals begin, continue the bride.

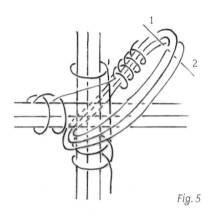

Fig. 5

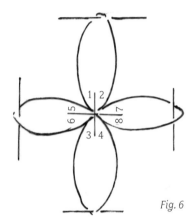

Fig. 6

PEARLS

Little pearls are often used in needle lace. They add a refined decoration when they are appliquéd to gaze items or other backgrounds. They can also be used as a connection between two separate motifs or between two rows of lace.

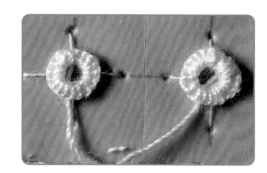

The method I'll be showing you was invented by Mrs. Boone (you can find it in her book *Siersteken in Naaldkant*). After several months of trying different methods, she mastered this technique, which has become a reference for all lace makers. It will allow you to make small, isolated pearls. To make pearls on a gaze background, we use the opening in the gaze and the surrounding stitches to attach the thread.

The pearls are worked using the same thread used for the lace.

This decoration is also used in bobbin lace. The Rosaline Perlée, for example (photos below), takes its name from this method. The pearls are made separately and then appliquéd to the lace.

Details of Rosaline lace (bobbin lace) decorated with needle lace pearls, from where the Rosaline Perlée lace takes its name.

HOW TO DO IT

1. Prepare your support and draw a horizontal line.

2. At the spots where you want to make your pearls, put in your stay stitches with fine thread. Do two horizontal stitches on the line, 1 cm apart, then do two vertical stay stitches on each side of the horizontal stitches (fig. 1).

3. At the intersection of the stay stitches, there is a small opening. This is the dimension of the pearl you are going to make. The smaller it is, the smaller the pearl will be.

4. Pull a thread around this space, passing it under the stay stitches, always working in the same direction. The number of passes will determine the volume of the pearl (fig. 2a and figs. 3 to 5).

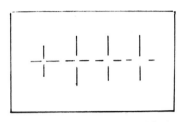

Fig. 1

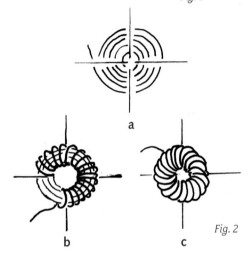

a

b   c

Fig. 2

5. When you have done the desired number of passes, topstitch the threads (fig. 2b and c).

6. To finish off, pass the working thread under the last topstitch to close the circle and use the rest of the thread to fix the pearl to the lace.

Fig. 3. The extremity of the starting thread is taken up in the topstitch.

Fig. 4

Fig. 5

WHEELS

Wheels are highly popular decorative elements. There are a large variety of wheels, just as there are limitless possibilities in interior decorating.

HOW TO DO IT

1. Prepare your support. Draw several circles, the same diameter, next to each other (the ones used here have a diameter of 13 mm).

2. Do your cordonnet, following the directions in figs. 1 and 2.

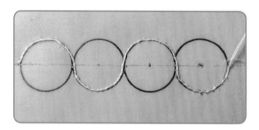

Fig. 1

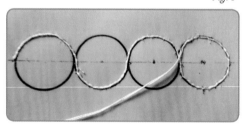

Fig. 2

Wheel 1

3. Do a row of Point de Tulle (see page 76) in the first circle (fig. 3). You can also fill the circle with buttonhole stitches.

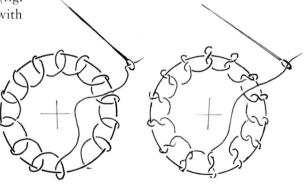

Buttonhole stitches   Point de Tulle

Fig. 3

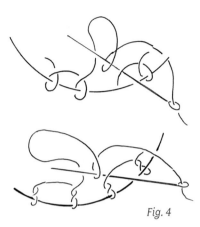

Fig. 4

4. Finish by passing the needle through the first Point de Tulle and fix the thread to the cordonnet (fig. 4).

5. Tack a small stay stitch cross in the middle of the wheel (fig. 5).

6. Overcast the loops in the preceding row to the beginning of the first petal.

7. Create the frame of the petals with two passes of thread. Pass the needle through one of the loops of the tulle to fix the top of the first petal. Pull the thread to the center and pass it under the stay stitch cross. Make the top petal by passing the thread through a loop to fix it. Pull the thread toward the center, crossing the petals in the direction of the arrows in fig. 5 and repeat the operation to double the thread.

8. Overcast the loops until you reach the place where the next petal will be. Repeat step 6. Choose the number of petals according to the size of the wheel, spacing them evenly (figs. 6 and 7).

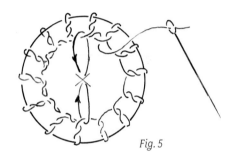

Fig. 5

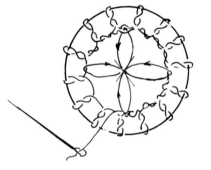

Fig 6. Wheel with 4 petals

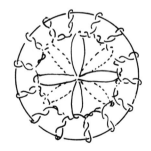

Fig 7. Wheel with 8 petals

Petal

If you want to do a lot of petals, make the circle large enough or use very fine thread.

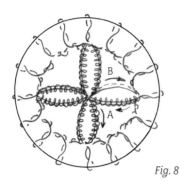

Fig. 8

9. Once the petals' frame is finished, topstitch them, starting at the top and working to the center. Be sure to take up the two threads in the topstitch (fig. 8).

10. At the end of each row of topstitching, pass the needle under the top to stop the loop from turning (see page 80).

Wheel 2

3. Inside one of the circles done in step 1, draw a concentric circle and four evenly spaced diameters (fig. 10).

4. Do a row of Point de Tulle attached to the cordonnet of the large circle.

5. Overcast the loops to the first diameter. Pull the thread, following fig. 9 and return to the center, overcasting the diameter.

6. Proceed in the same way for the next three diameters (fig. 10).

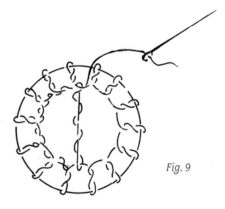

Fig. 9

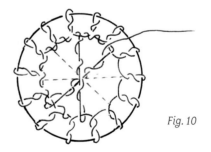

Fig. 10

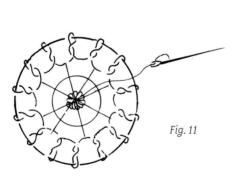

Fig. 11

7. After bringing the thread back to the center, make the pearl (see page 90) in the center of the circles (fig. 11).

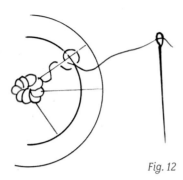

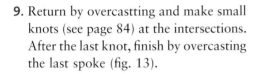

Fig. 12

8. Mark the place for the knots at the junction of the interior circle and the diameters. Pull the thread to one of them (fig. 12) and make a loop.

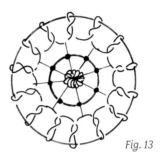

Fig. 13

9. Return by overcastting and make small knots (see page 84) at the intersections. After the last knot, finish by overcasting the last spoke (fig. 13).

Wheel 3

This variant is the same as wheel 2, without the small knots.

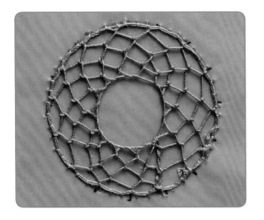

DECORATIVE NET

For this rather modern pattern, your usual lace thread is okay, but it's better to use 80 DMC thread.

HOW TO DO IT

1. Draw a circle (the one shown has a diameter of 3 cm; fig. 1). Do your cordonnet and then do the first row in large buttonhole stitches, spacing them evenly (fig. 2). For the following rows, do large buttonhole stitches, passing through the loops in the preceding row each time.

2. At the last row, overcast all the loops and pull the thread to tighten them (fig. 2).

3. Finish by overcasting each loop up to the cordonnet (fig. 3).

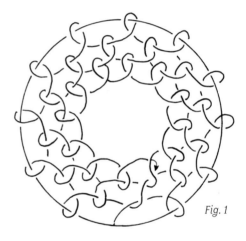

Fig. 1

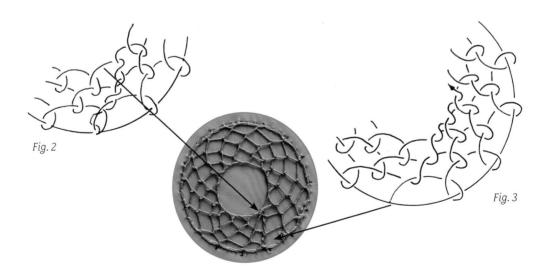

Fig. 2

Fig. 3

SMALL ROSES

This decorative element that you find in modern lacework is really pretty between two circles. It can also be used in other shapes.

HOW TO DO IT

1. Prepare your support by drawing a circle (the one shown here has a diameter of 3 cm). Do your cordonnet. Do a first row of large buttonhole stitches, the same as for the decorative net, making sure they are evenly spaced.

2. 1st row: Do a rose around each buttonhole stitch. To do this, start from the last stitch and make circles around the stitch, passing alternatively over and under the cordonnet. Keep the threads flat, avoiding superimposing the other circles. Finish the rose by passing the needle underneath and overcast the cordonnet to the next rose.

3. 2nd row: After the last rose of the first row, do a row of buttonhole stitches, taking up the loops in the preceding row, and then do your roses (you can do several rows or just one, according to your pattern).

4. At the end of the last row, pass the needle under one of the roses and pull the thread back to the cordonnet.

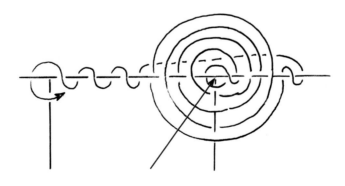

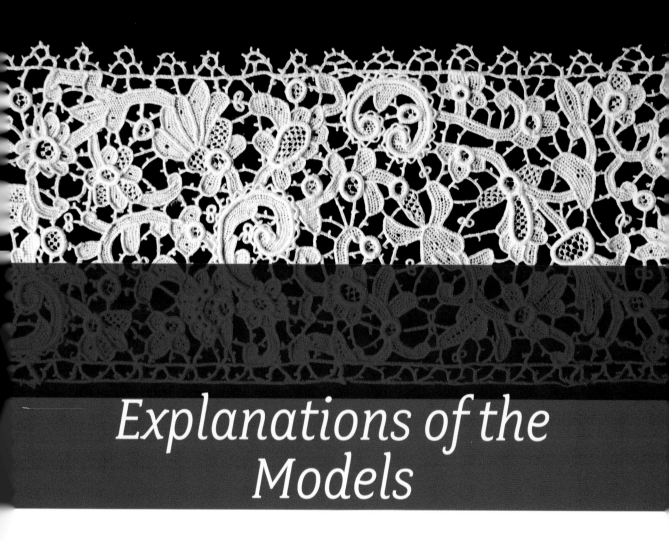

Explanations of the Models

Small Flower

This first model is easy to make and can be used as a broach. Prepare your support carefully (see page 33).

Material
- White Dare-Dare 50/2 cotton thread
- 100 Brok fine thread (for the cordonnet)
- Absorbent cotton
- Fine metallic thread (optional)

Points used
- Close gaze (p. 48)
- Simple pea (p. 69)
- Point de Tulle (p. 76)
- Topstitch (p. 50)
- Topstitch with picots (p. 52)

THE PETALS

1. Measure the dimension of the thread for the cordonnet on the pattern, taking into account where you will be branching off (fig. 1). In the sketch, branching off is in green and going back is in red. Multiply the result by two to get the length of the thread for the cordonnet.

2. Do the cordonnet in one single operation (see page 34), following the arrows in the sketch and the order in which they are carried out:
Start with A. Stitch the small circle and fix it to the starting stitch. From there do B and then go one to 1. Branch off toward the circle "A," using one thread (see page 37).

Return toward 2 with the two threads. At each change of direction, take only one thread; take it to the edge of the row and return with the two threads.

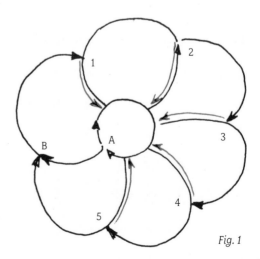

Fig. 1

3. Start the lacework by following the direction of the dotted line (fig. 2). The vertical lines give the petals a closed aspect, while the horizontal lines give them an open aspect.
Do three petals in close gaze (see page 48) and three in simple pea (see page 69).

4. Do the topstitching following the same direction as the cordonnet. Do topstitching with picots (see page 52) on the outer contour, three picots on each petal, evenly separated. Remove the flower from its support and do the finishing touches (trimming and smoothing). The flower is ready for its heart.

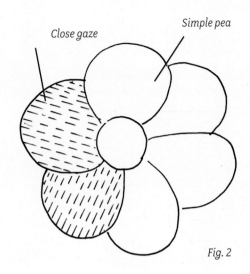

Close gaze *Simple pea*

Fig. 2

Metallic thread

You can put metallic thread in your topstitch (for the outer contour, not where you branched off). In this case, use three filler yarn threads instead of four. Shape the metallic thread at the start of where you branched off, and block the end of it (since it has a tendency to slip) by pinning the end to the cloth (see the sketch below).

You can find different-colored metallic thread in craft stores.

metallic thread *filler yarn threads*

THE HEART

5. Draw a circle with a diameter of 16 mm and do the cordonnet.

6. Do the first row in Point de Tulle (see page 76) around the circumference.

7. Do the interior of the circle in close gaze (see page 48) in the direction shown by the dotted lines (fig. 3).

8. Don't topstitch the heart. Remove the lace and do the finishing touches. Pass a thread through the loops of the Point

de Tulle, pull them close, stuff the heart with absorbent cotton and then sew it to the center of the flower.

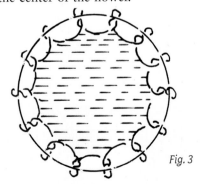

Fig. 3

Fish

This pattern blends different previously detailed fillings and modes. It can be applied to clothing as an ornament or to paper to make small greeting cards.

Material

- DMC 6-strand floss : orange No. 721, red No. 350, sky blue No. 162, pink No. 224 and blue No. 806
- 100 Brok fine thread (for the cordonnet)
- Pattern of the fish (page 118)

Points used

- Point de Tulle (p. 76)
- Close gaze (p. 48)
- Simple pea (p. 69)
- Topstitch (p. 50)
- Pearls (p. 90)

Colored lace

If the lace is in different colors, the cordonnet must be the same color, especially the places along the cordonnet where there are no topstitches. To change colors in the middle of the work, superimpose two threads of the desired color parallel to the precedents. Topstitch these four threads together (two stitches) and then cut the old threads. Continue with the new color. The same procedure is carried out for the finishing topstitching.

THE CORDONNET

1. Measure the dimension of the thread for the cordonnet on the pattern, taking into account where you will be branching off (fig. 1). Multiply the result by two to get the length of the thread for the cordonnet.

2. Following fig. 1 start the cordonnet at "A" and continue to "B," taking into account the outline of the fin. Branch off and come back between "B" and "C."

3. Continue the cordonnet, following the arrow from "B" to "D" and then to "E." Branch off and come back between "E" and "D." Continue to "F" and "A" and then branch off and come back between "A" and "F."

THE LACE

4. Start the lacework, following the direction of the dotted lines. Do the fish's tail in Point de Tulle (see page 76) and the narrow part in close gaze (see page 48). The body is done in simple pea (see page 69).

5. Do the fins in Point de Tulle and the mouth in close gaze.

6. Finish by topstitching (see page 50) along the outer contour of the fish, following the same direction as the cordonnet.

7. Do pearls (see page 90) for the eye and the bubbles.

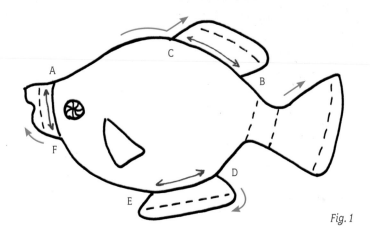

Fig. 1

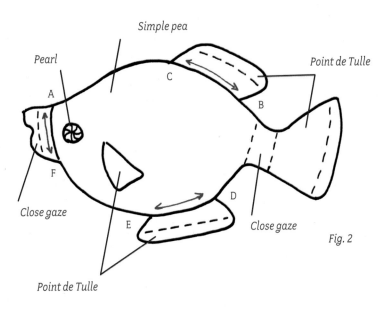

Fig. 2

Oak Leaves and Acorns

This pattern with its autumnal colors can be appliquéd to clothing or to tulle. As with the fish in the previous pages, you can fix it to a thick piece of paper to make a greeting card.

Material

- DMC 6-strand floss : brown No. 680, medium olive-green No. 733, green No. 991 and dark hunter green No. 3345
- 100 Brok fine thread (for the cordonnet)
- Pattern (page 118)

Points used

- Close Gaze (p. 48)
- Fly (p. 59)
- Simple pea (p. 69)
- Point de Tulle (p. 76)
- Topstitch (p. 50)

THE CORDONNET

1. Measure the dimension of the thread for the cordonnet on the pattern, taking into account where you will be branching off (fig. 1). Multiply the result by two to get the length of the thread for the cordonnet.

2. Following fig. 1, start the cordonnet from "A" toward "B" and carry on to "C" (outer cordonnet). Branch off and come back between "C" and "B," following the arrow in the sketch, then return to "A" to make the left side of the first cup. Continue toward "F," "D," and "E."

3. Work on the central vein from "E" to "D" and the small veins by successively branching off on the way back down.

4. When you reach "E" again, continue toward "G," "H," and "I" (outer cordonnet). Branch off and come back between "I" and "H" and finish the second cup at "G." Finish the cordonnet by returning to "A."

THE LACE

5. Do the lacework, following the direction of the dotted lines in fig. 1 and following the points indicated. For the leaf, do a row of Point de Tulle (see page 76) along the small veins and do the rest in close gaze.

6. Finish by topstitching (see page 50), following the same direction as the cordonnet.

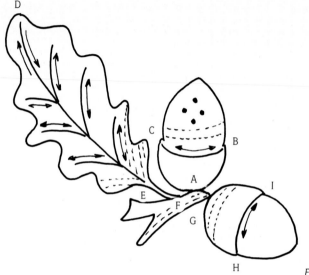

Fig. 1

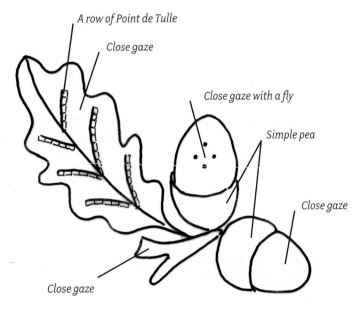

A row of Point de Tulle

Close gaze

Close gaze with a fly

Simple pea

Close gaze

Close gaze

Fig. 2

Coaster

This circular lacework is a good exercise. It can be used as it is as a coaster or as an appliquéd ornament.

Material

- White Dare-Dare 50/2 cotton thread
- 100 Brok fine thread (for the cordonnet)
- Pattern (page 118)

Points used

- Point de Tulle (p. 76)
- Close gaze (p. 48)
- Wide gaze (p. 49)
- Fly (p. 59)
- Bride (p. 78)
- Topstitch (p. 50)
- Stars (p. 87)

THE CORDONNET

1. Do the cordonnet for the contours of the three circles.

2. Measure the contour of the flower, taking into account branching off (fig. 1). Multiply the result by two to get the length of the thread for the cordonnet.

3. Do the cordonnet for the flower, starting with the center. Work following the number in fig. 1: first 1 to 4, then return to 1, attach the thread to the cordonnet, and go from 1 toward 5; continue to 12. Don't forget where to branch off and come back between the flower and the center.

4. Using fine thread, place the eight crossed stay stitches (A) and the 16 fixing stitches (B) for the stars (fig. 1).

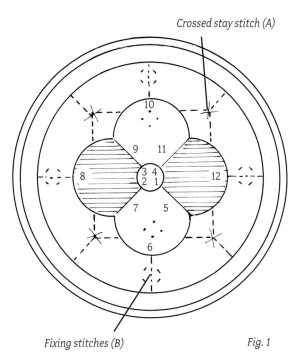

Crossed stay stitch (A)

Fixing stitches (B)

Fig. 1

From the largest to the smallest

When we have a pattern made up of several concentric circles, we generally start with the one on the outside; that is to say, the largest circle.

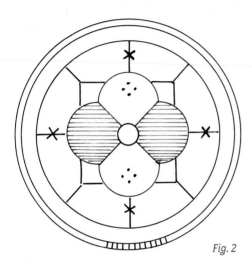

Fig. 2

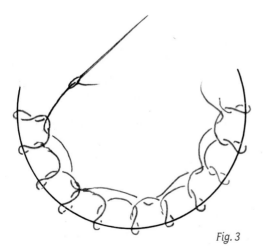

Fig. 3

THE LACE

5. 1st row: Do a first row of Point de Tulle (see page 76), working from left to right between the first two circles (fig. 2).

6. 2nd row: Do a row of close gaze (see page 48). Once you have come back to the starting point, start again in the opposite direction (from right to left). Pull the working thread and attach it to the loops in the previous row, overcasting about every 2 cm (fig. 3).

7. 3rd row: Do a row of close gaze from left to right. Skip a stitch from time to time to reduce the circumference of the circle. The decrease in the number of loops depends on your work, so take this into account. Continue in this way to make the filling between the two circles.

8. Do the fillings of each petal of the flower: two in close gaze, working from the exterior of the petal toward the heart, with a central fly (see page 59); the two other petals in wide gaze (see page 49), in the previous direction (fig. 2).

9. Do the brides: pull three threads under the crossed stay stitches to make the bride (see page 78) and the stars (see page 87).

10. Continue by doing the topstitching of the exterior and the interior circles (see page 50). Note: There aren't any topstitches between the row of tulle and the close gaze. Finish by doing the topstitching on the flower, following the same direction as the cordonnet.

Sail Boat

This creation takes into account a large number of points already detailed. You can choose to copy this pattern faithfully or do the fillings and modes according to your preferences.

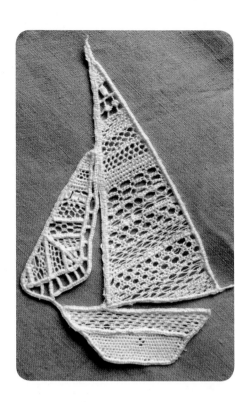

Material
- White Dare-Dare 50/2 cotton thread
- 100 Brok fine thread (for the cordonnet)
- Horsehair
- Sailboat pattern (p. 118)

Points used
- See the legend for fig. 2 on pages 110–111

THE CORDONNET

1. With fine thread, do the crosses necessary for the brides (see page 78).

2. Prepare the length of thread for the cordonnet, following the lines of the pattern and taking into account branching off. Multiply the result by two to get the length of the thread for the cordonnet.

3. Using fig. 1, do the cordonnet, following the arrows from "A" toward "B."

Continue to "C," then do the first branching off along the horizontal lines of the sail (see page 37).

4. Take up the two threads and continue toward "D," doing the successive branching off along the horizontal lines. Continue toward "A," "E," "L," and "M". When you reach "N" branch off and come back. Continue to "O" and finish at "A."

Trick

Wind each of the two cordonnet threads around a small piece of numbered card, to take up a different thread for each branching off. For example, the first branching off is done with thread 1 and the second with thread 2 and so on. The length of the thread is thereby evenly distributed (this procedure is used where there is much branching off).

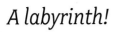

A labyrinth!

Working the cordonnet might seem very complex, but it will be more solid if it is done from beginning to end in a single pass. Follow precisely the direction shown.

5. Do the jib's cordonnet with new thread. Start at "E," fixing the thread to the hull. Go toward "F," "G," "H," and "I." Go up toward "J" and the "K" with one thread, leaving the other at "I." At "K" do the first branching off, come back, and go down toward "J," branching off at the horizontal lines. At "J" branch off and come back toward "G." Work toward "I," branching off on the vertical lines of the sail. At "I," take up the thread you left there and finish at "F."

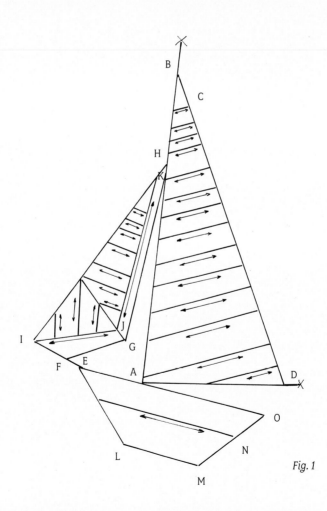

Fig. 1

THE LACE

6. Start the lace with Point d'Esprit (see page 86) and small knots (see page 84). You can reproduce identical modes shown in fig. 2.

7. Work the topstitching (see page 50), following the same direction as the cordonnet, adding four threads and a horsehair. Before starting, wind the topstitch threads two by two around two pieces of numbered card to divide the lengths of thread evenly when branching off (see the trick in step 1).

8. The brides are worked at the same time as the topstitching. To begin the decorative bride at "B" to the crossed stay stitch, pull three threads and work according to the instructions on page 78. Continue topstitching afterward.
Do the same for "D" and the jib's brides: stop topstitching and work the bride.

Jib

1. Close gaze

2. Point de Tulle

3. Buttonhole with cord (3)

4. Point d'Esprit

5. Point de Tulle

6. Buttonhole without a cord (3)

7. Buttonhole without a cord (18)

8. Point de Tulle

9. Buttonhole without a cord (12)

10. Point de Tulle

Hull

1. Close gaze

2. Fly

3. Wide gaze

Sail

4. Buttonhole with cord (1)

5. Buttonhole with cord (2)

6. Simple pea

7. Buttonhole with cord (1)

8. Simple pea

9. Buttonhole with cord (2)

10. Buttonhole without a cord (4)

11. Buttonhole with cord (3)

12. Point de Tulle

13. Buttonhole without a cord (2)

14. Zigzag

15. Small knots

16. Point d'Esprit

17. Close gaze

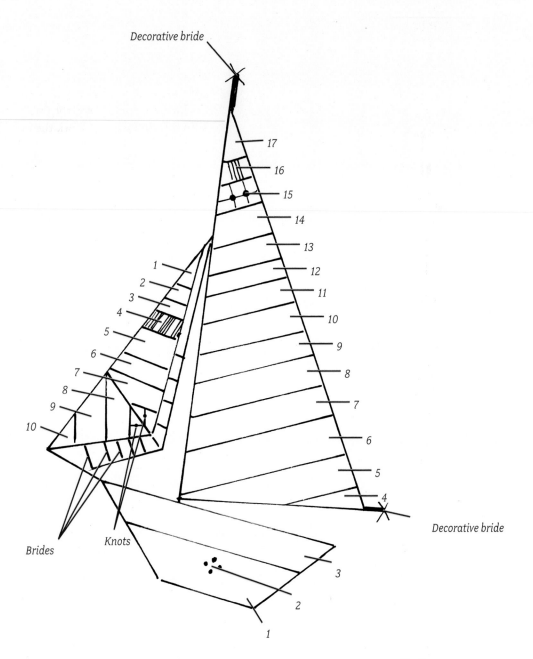

Decorative bride

17
16
15
14
13
12
11
10
9
8
7
6
5
4

Decorative bride

1
2
3
4
5
6
7
8
9
10

Brides

Knots

1
2
3

Fig. 2

Flower with Added Petals & Butterfly

This piece is composed of two main motifs, a flower and a butterfly. The elements added on (two petals and the butterfly's wing) are fixed while working the topstitch, adding bulk to the lace, which makes it more lifelike.

Material

- Indian silk floss
- 100 Brok fine thread (for the cordonnet)
- Pattern of the flower (p. 119)
- Pattern of the butterfly (p. 119)

Points used

- Close gaze (p. 48)
- Small knots (p. 84)
- Point de Tulle (p. 76)
- Fly (p. 59)
- Point d' Esprit (p. 86)
- Simple pea (p. 69)
- Pearls (p. 90)
- Bride (p. 78)
- Topstitch (p. 50)

THE FLOWER

1. Measure the contours and the lines inside the pattern, starting with "A" (fig. 1). Count branching off. Multiply the result and add on a couple of centimeters. Wind each length of thread around numbered cards to avoid using the same thread for branching off (see page 108) (fig. 2).

2. Using fine thread, place the stay stitches for the small knots represented by crosses in fig. 1.

3. Start the cordonnet at "A," working toward "B," "C," "E," and "D." Go down the length of the main vein in the leaf from "D" to "C," using a single thread, and go back up, branching off along the small veins. Follow the arrows in fig. 1.

4. Continue with two threads toward "E," "F," "G," and "H." Branch off and come back between "H" and "K," passing by "I." Returning to "H," continue to "J" with two threads. Then branch off and come back along the veins from "I" to "J." Return toward "K" and then "L." Then work toward "M."

5. Branch off and come back between "M" and "N," passing through "O." Work toward "P," "Q," "R," and "S." Branch off and come back between "S" and "W." Return to "S" and work

toward "T." Branch off and come back between "T" and "W." Continue from "T" to "U." Branch off and come back twice between "U" and "W" to shape the petals. Continue to "V," branching off and coming back four times toward "X" for the top petals. Returning to "V," work toward V1. Work the small circles, following the red arrows for the forward stitches and the green for returning, and then continue by branching off and coming back between "W" and "V." Returning to "V," shape the next two petals by branching off and coming back from "W." Continue toward "Y." Branch off and come back twice toward "W."

6. Return to "Y" and continue to "Z" and from there to "a." Work in the same way as the previous leaf, going up the large vein to "P." Attach the thread to the cordonnet at "P" and branch off for the small veins on the way back down.

7. Return to "a" and work toward "b." Branch off and come back between "b" and "O." Continue toward "c" and "d." Work the veins in the same way as before and finish at "A."

Fig. 1

Fig. 2

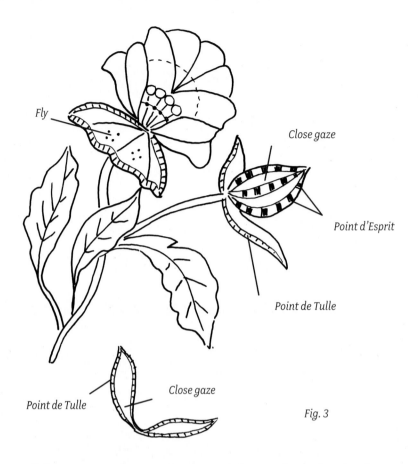

Fly

Close gaze

Point d'Esprit

Point de Tulle

Point de Tulle

Close gaze

Fig. 3

8. Start with the small knots (see page 84) and Point d'Esprit (see page 86), following figs. 2 and 3.

9. Work the lace in whichever order you prefer, respecting the direction of the rows (figs. 3 to 7).

10. Around the petals, under the flower, and under the bud, do a row of Point de Tulle before doing the filling (figs. 3 to 6).

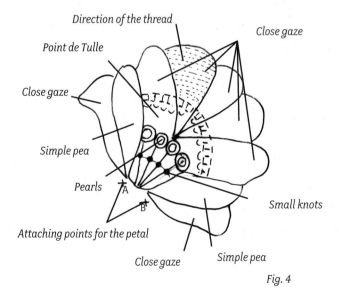

Direction of the thread

Point de Tulle

Close gaze

Close gaze

Simple pea

Pearls

Attaching points for the petal

Close gaze

Simple pea

Small knots

Fig. 4

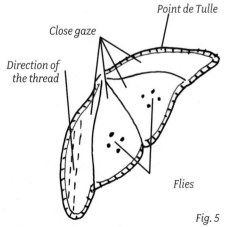

Close gaze

Point de Tulle

Direction of the thread

Flies

Fig. 5

114

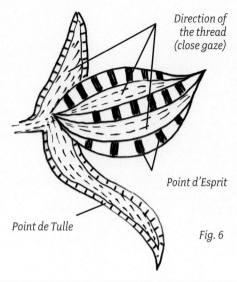

Direction of the thread (close gaze)

Point d'Esprit

Point de Tulle

Fig. 6

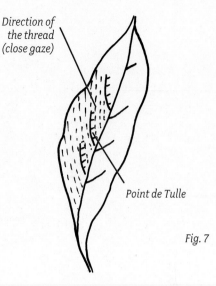

Direction of the thread (close gaze)

Point de Tulle

Fig. 7

11. On the leaves, do a row of Point de Tulle along the small veins (fig. 7) and then work the interior in close gaze (see page 48)

12. When the lace is finished, work on the topstitching, following the same direction as the cordonnet, leaving a space in the topstitching between the two red crosses as in fig. 1.

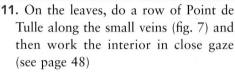

THE PETALS

13. Do the cordonnet around the two independent petals, starting in the hollow part (fig. 1).

14. Work the lace, doing a row of Point de Tulle around the contour and the interior in close gaze (fig. 8).

15. Topstitch the petals. You can replace

the horsehair by metallic thread, which will allow you to shape them (see page 101). Stop the topstitch between points "A1" and "B1"; leave this space free (fig. 1). Leave the threads in place.

16. Remove the lace from its support (see page 42) and then, taking up the topstitch threads left in place, continue topstitching, fixing the petals to the heart of the flower. For this, superimpose the petals on the flower, matching the points "A1" and "B1" to the red crosses in the heart of the flower (fig. 1), and continue topstitching the place between "A1" and "B1."
You will now have three-dimensional petals that stand out from the flower.

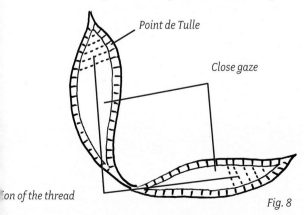

Point de Tulle

Close gaze

...on of the thread

Fig. 8

THE BUTTERFLY

17. Measure the contour of the pattern to prepare your cordonnet thread, in the same way for the previous lacework. Using fine thread, put in the crossed stay stitches at the ends of the legs and antennae (fig. 9). These will be worked as brides, at the same time as the topstitches.

18. Start the cordonnet at "A" toward "B." Branch off and come back between "A" and "B," passing by "C."

19. Starting at "B," work toward "D," "E," and "F." Branch off and come back between "F" and "G" and then between "F" and "C." Continue, branching off between "F" and "A." From "F," work toward "H" and then finish at "B."

20. Work the lace, following fig. 10.

21. Finish by topstitching, following the direction of the cordonnet, except for the section between "F" and "A," which you will leave to one side. Work the brides for the legs and antennae at the same time as topstitching.

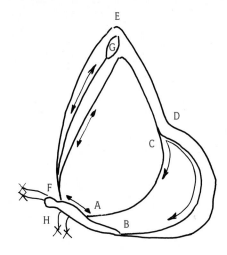

Fig. 9

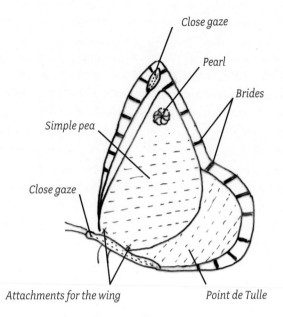

Close gaze

Pearl

Brides

Simple pea

Close gaze

Attachments for the wing

Point de Tulle

Fig. 10

THE BUTTERFLY'S WING

22. Do the wing's cordonnet by working from "A1" to "B1" and then on to "C1." Return to "A1," branch off and come back between "A1" and "B1" for the inner cordonnet.

23. Work the lace following fig. 11.

24. Start the topstitching at "A1" toward "B1" and branch off and come back between "B1" and "A1" for the inner cordonnet. Return to "B1" and continue to "C1." Leave the topstitches between "C1" and "A1" aside for the moment.

25. In the same way as for the petals, remove the lace from its support. Superimpose the butterfly, making sure

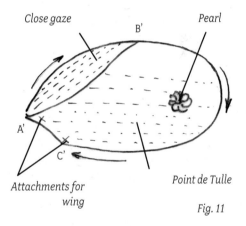

Close gaze

B'

Pearl

A'

C'

Attachments for wing

Point de Tulle

Fig. 11

that the points "F" and "A" correspond (fig. 9) to the points "A1" and "C1" of the wing (fig. 11). Fix the parts by working the topstitches between the two parts left aside. For this, use the topstitch threads from the butterfly's wing (see page 116).

$\mathfrak{S}$ketches of the Models

Life size

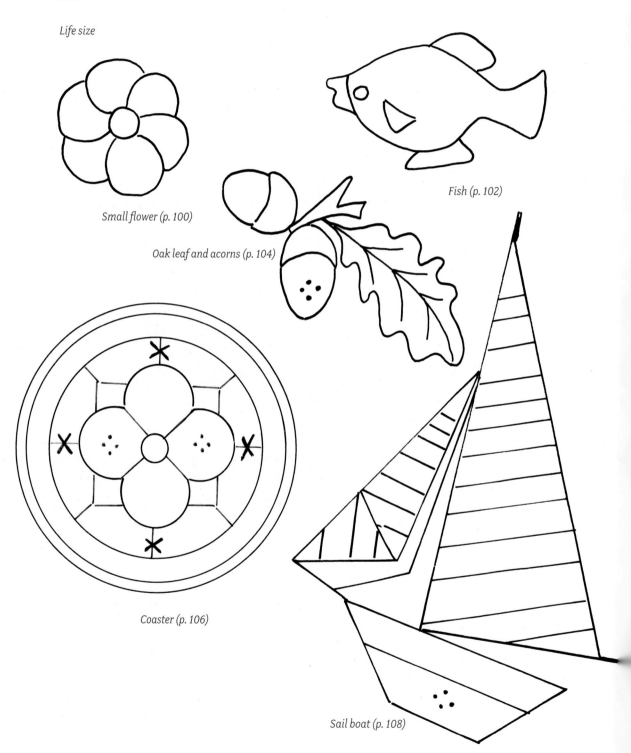

Small flower (p. 100)

Fish (p. 102)

Oak leaf and acorns (p. 104)

Coaster (p. 106)

Sail boat (p. 108)

Flower with added petals
(p. 112)

Butterfly with added wing (p. 116)

Author's Gallery

Competition based on the theme "Five Roses," carried out in bobbin lace and needle lace. First prize in the competition Grand Couvige international de la dentelle in Puy-en-Velay (October 2011).

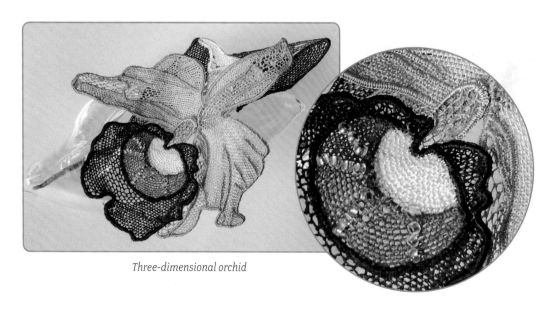

Three-dimensional orchid

Modern lacework called "Actinie." End-of-thesis work-based project (2006).

Three-dimensional hat representing France at the OIDFA Congress in Adelaide, Australia (2014)

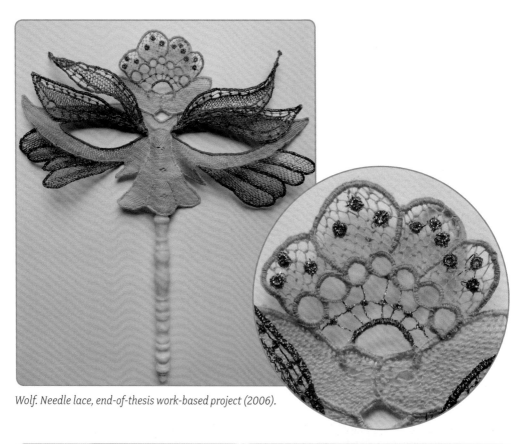

Wolf. Needle lace, end-of-thesis work-based project (2006).

Pierrot and Colombine. Small tableau for a child's bedroom.

Cornflower and poppy, four o'clock flower and honeysuckle (from left to right). Lace inspired by "Fleurs aimées," by J.J. Grandville (1846).

Bibliography

Please note that I learned this craft from lace makers in France, which is why the book's bibliography contains French references.

Boone Irma, *Siersteken in naaldkant*, Artistic School for Needle lace, Nr D/3899/n° 1, 1990.

Bruggeman Martine, *L'Europe de la dentelle*, Stichting-Kunstboek, Bruges, 1997.

Bury-Palliser Fanny, *Histoire de la dentelle*, Firmin-Didot, Paris, 1890.

Charles Marguerite et Pagès Louis, *Les broderies et les dentelles*, Félix Juven, Paris, 1905.

Delesques-Dépalle Brigitte, *La dentelle à l'aiguille*, Créer, Nonette, 1994.

Desmettre Bérengère, *La dentelle d'Alençon*, Éditions de Saxe, Lyon, 2012.

Dillmont Thérèse de, *Encyclopédie des ouvrages de dames*, DMC Library new edition by Solar, Paris, 2013.

Dillmont Thérèse de, *La dentelle renaissance*, DMC Library, Mulhouse, 1920.

Fouriscot Mick, *Le secret des dentelles*, vol. 1, 2 et 3, Éditions Carpentier, Paris, 1998, 2000 et 2003.

Huijben Anny & Van den Kieboom Ineke, *Naaldkant*, Uitgeverij Terra, 1988.

Lefébure Ernest, *Broderies et dentelles*, Ernest Gründ, new edition added to by Auguste Lefébure, Paris, 1922.

Paulis L., *Pour connaître la dentelle*, Nederlandsche Boekhandel, Anvers, 1947.

Paulis L., *Les points à l'aiguille belges*, Royal Museums of Art and History, Brussels, 1947.

Les points à l'aiguille du xvie au xxe siècle, exposition catalogue, Hôtel de la Dentelle, Brioude, 2014.

Tracy G. M., *Dentelles et dentellières de France*, Didier, Paris, 1946.

Trésors du musée des Beaux-Arts et de la Dentelle, « Faisons le Point. Le fil de l'excellence », Alençon, vol. 3, 2012.

Acknowledgments

With thanks:

To Bernard, my husband who encouraged me over several years to write this book and who helped me with a lot of good advice;

To my needle lace students, and particularly Marie-Chantale Leblanc, who gave me the benefit of her knowledge in editing;

To Madame Johanna Allouch, curator and director of the musée des Beaux-Arts et de la Dentelle d'Alençon, who gave me permission to take the photos used in my book;

To Madame Paola Toselli in Burano, who happily showed me her private collection;

To Monsieur Hervé Chevrier, archivist and secretary of the Société des Sciences de l'Yonne, for his numerous encouragements;

To my editor, Anne Le Bras, who had confidence in me and without whom this book wouldn't exist;

To the team at Editions Eyrolles, and notably Anaïs Nectoux for her patient collaboration;

And finally to my needle lace teachers, Mesdames Geneviève Leplat and Hilda Vrijsen.

Heritage Crochet in a New Light: Enriching Your Designs with Heirloom Lace Techniques

RITA DE MAINTENON
978-0-7643-5347-5

Learn how to use heritage crochet techniques to enrich any crochet project. Clear instructions from master teacher Rita de Maintenon, plus helpful online videos and 160 photos, allow you to master and combine broomstick, hairpin, and Tunisian lace, plus Aran cables, Irish crochet, and thread lace. For intermediate level crocheters.

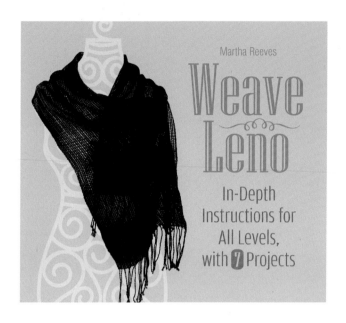

Weave Leno: In-Depth Instructions for All Levels, with 7 Projects

MARTHA REEVES
978-0-7643-5101-3

Master and enjoy the intricate leno weave with this comprehensive guide. For new weavers and advanced-level weavers alike, it offers practical instructions and "secret" tips resulting from Reeves's years of research and sampling. Colorful photos, step-by-step instructions, and seven beautiful projects teach leno pick up, bead leno, Tarascan lace, and more.